LETTERS
TO
GABRIEL

The true story of
Gabriel Michael Santorum

LETTERS
TO
GABRIEL

The true story of
Gabriel Michael Santorum
by Karen Garver Santorum

IGNATIUS PRESS

All Scripture References are from
the New American Bible unless otherwise noted.

At the Death of a Child by Donald Deffner,
Copyright 1993 by Concordia Publishing House.
Used with permission.

Cover design by Riz Boncan Marsella
Cover art from gettyimages.com

For my husband, Rick, and our dear children, Elizabeth, John, Daniel, Sarah Maria, Peter, Patrick, and Isabella. I thank God every day for blessing me with your beautiful lives!

Special thanks to my parents for their constant love and support over the years.

Note from the Publisher

During the 1980 campaign for the presidency of the United States, there was a moment that threatened to unleash a national controversy over the separation of church and state.

The fiery and provocative Evangelical pastor and preacher James Robison had organized a National Affairs Briefing of the Religious Roundtable in Dallas, Texas, on August 28, 1980, late in the campaign. 15,000 Christian conservatives attended, and presidential candidate Governor Ronald Reagan was invited to speak.

As Reagan approached the podium there was apprehension in the audience and latent hostility in many of the media representatives covering the event. Reagan defused the tension immediately with his now famous introductory remark: "I know that you can't endorse me...but I endorse you."

Ignatius Press is a Catholic publisher and this book is being republished in the midst of another presidential campaign, the campaign of 2012. The book was written by the wife of one of the candidates, Rick Santorum, and first published in 1998. Because of the increased public visibility of Senator Santorum and his family during the campaign, there has been a growing number of people asking for this book.

Because we think this book is such a beautiful testimony to the worth and dignity of very human life, we want to respond to the many requests for it. Still, following the wise example of Ronald Reagan, we know that we can't endorse Rick Santorum. But we do endorse his wife, Karen Garver Santorum, and the pro-life, pro-family principles she expresses so movingly in this book.

Letters to Gabriel is about the Santorum's third child, Gabriel Michael, who died shortly after birth.

Fr. Joseph Fessio, S.J.
Ignatius Press

Foreword

Every human life, from the oldest adult to the very

youngest unborn child, is a gift of God ~ to love and be loved.

Gabriel Michael Santorum, living only a couple of hours after

his premature birth, is a gift of God, and I recommend that

these letters from the loving heart of a mother be read because

they remind us of God's tender love for us expressed by Isaiah,

Can a mother forget her infant,

be without tenderness for the child in her womb?

(Isaiah 49:15)

May God bless Richard and Karen Santorum,

the parents of little Gabriel Michael, and console them with the

knowledge that their son is in Heaven with God. May Mary,

the Mother of Jesus, use these

inspiring letters to encourage all expectant mothers

to cherish the gift of life they carry,

and to love the child within their womb.

Let us pray   *God bless you*
*   M.C. Teresa. mc*

-Mother Teresa of Calcutta
June 18, 1997

Introduction

"Why am I living?" Not many people have the guts to say it out loud, but lots of us think it. There's a slew of self-help books, mid-day talk shows, and one-hour counseling services to help us find meaning and purpose. Sometimes the purpose is hard to pin down in this no-deposit-no-return culture.

But Rick and Karen Santorum have no trouble with that. For them, purpose and meaning are all wrapped up in one simple value: all life is sacred. They learned that when they lost their child Gabriel to a severe disability. And the value was reinforced again when Bella was born.

This little girl has Trisomy 18, a genetic disorder similar to Down Syndrome but more serious. There have been some who have looked at the Santorums and thought, Isn't this child better off dead than disabled? Rick and Karen certainly don't believe so!

They see a bigger picture. Bella, to them, is a treasure, and God has given her to Rick and Karen and the family to be nurtured and cared for. In so doing, the family unit is strengthened, sacrifice and love are honored, commitment is extolled, and their example influences thousands of other special needs families across this nation to do the same.

The Santorums also understand that if the rights of a child with a disability are not safeguarded, then it spells danger for all people who are medically fragile, whether young or old. When God is removed from the public arena—when he and his precepts are ignored anywhere around the world—it spells danger for the unborn child, the newborn with disabilities, those in comas, and the elderly. People are not "better off dead than disabled", but if this growing premise is not opposed, personhood and human dignity will be systematically targeted and dismantled, all for the sake of cost and convenience.

This is the way it is in a post-modern world played out on the landscape of disability. Some have looked at children like Bella and said, "Pull out her feeding tube. Even if that does violate her rights, the little girl lacks any cognitive capacity to experience any kind of dignity." But do you see the logical outcome of such a statement? If we follow this post-modern perspective, then we should let the Alzheimer patient run around without clothes on...let the intellectually disabled teenager eat off the ground...allow the child with autism to flap his arms all day repeatedly with no intervention. This is where post-modern logic concerning disabilities will lead us.

But God has called us to treat Bella—and millions like her—with respect and human dignity. God has called us to secure her rights and to ascribe positive value to her disability. People deserve to be treated with dignity, even if—and especially if—that individual has no idea what human dignity looks or feels like.

This book you hold in your hands, *Letters to Gabriel*, is a clarion call to every American. We need to treat people not as things, but as individuals with inherent worth, no matter how severe the disabling condition. Together we must spread the word that as the moral fabric in our society wears thin, no one is more in jeopardy than those who are too weak, too small, or too elderly to grasp how dangerous the battle is. This is why I'm so grateful you are reading Rick and Karen's story....

Perhaps God is calling you to shape the future, for as Proverbs 31:9 says, "Speak up and judge fairly; defend the rights of the poor and needy." Even in your own neighborhood, you can advocate for those who are elderly, disabled or medically fragile. History shows that given the opportunity, society will move in the direction of convenience for the masses at the expense of the weak and vulnerable. Let's not treat people as things, but as human beings that bear the precious imprint of our great Creator God.

It's something Gabriel and Bella have taught us.

Joni Eareckson Tada
Joni and Friends International Disability Center
Spring 2012

A note to the reader....

*T*his book is a series of letters I wrote to my son, Gabriel Michael, who was born prematurely and died two hours after birth.

Some of these letters were written during my pregnancy and as events were occurring, in hopes that Gabriel would survive and that I could someday give him a detailed account of the miracle of his life. Others were written during the many sleepless nights that came after his death. I felt a terrible emptiness after the loss of my baby, and these written expressions were a part of my healing process. I also wanted to continue writing everything down so that years from now my husband, our children, and I will remember every detail of little Gabriel's life.

The bulk of these letters were never written for publication. I tucked them safely away in a drawer and planned to read them from time to time. The idea to publish began when I handed the letters over to my parents and a friend, and those readers encouraged me to publish.

At first, the thought of revealing an extremely personal event and exposing my pain, and that of my family's, simply was not a possibility. I constantly seek and protect the privacy of our family because of my husband's role as a United States Senator and the public life it creates.

Slowly, however, I began to see some merit in the publication of these letters. In reflecting on the life and death of Gabriel, I realized our story might illuminate in a personal way two compelling, human paradoxes.

The first is the paradox of suffering. Suffering and grief are at once universal and intensely individual. No one on this earth escapes suffering. At the same time, responses to it vary with each person. And no matter how much we might know that others have suffered similar losses, intense grief is often isolating and lonely.

I know that my husband and I were enormously comforted and strengthened by the personal expressions of so many other parents who shared their stories of grief in books and in personal letters to us. Each story was individual, but each contained shards of truth and hope. These shards helped us rebuild the wholeness of our daily lives. Precisely because the experience of grief is so individual, we were greatly helped by learning how others responded to grief and transcended it.

So after much thought and many prayers, I decided to share our story because I believe and hope it will help others. If sharing this story can comfort other parents in their grief, then revealing this very personal part of our lives is worth any loss of privacy.

The second paradox of our story, I believe, is the Christian paradox itself: In order to have life, we must lose it. Gabriel's death came upon the heels of the partial birth abortion debate in Congress—a debate in which my husband had played a prominent role. We learned when I was carrying Gabriel that he was a very sick baby and would not live long after birth. Thus we faced circumstances similar to those of many parents who choose an abortion—and in the later stages, a partial birth abortion—rather than allow a pregnancy to proceed.

For us, however, there was no choice. We never for a moment considered an abortion, although for legal reasons our doctors had to inform us that this was an option. We proceeded in what seemed to us to be the only way possible: We allowed Gabriel to live out the short life God gave him. He was born prematurely and was too young to survive for longer than two hours. He died naturally and peacefully in our arms, experiencing our love.

And so this is the other very individual reason why I wanted to tell Gabriel's story. If parents facing similar, heart-wrenching circumstances can take enough strength and hope from this story to embrace life, then our loss can be transmuted into new life. Through the story of Gabriel's death, perhaps others can live.

In the account that follows, I offer no theories, no analysis of grief, no simple solutions to human loss and suffering. I offer only this—the story of my son and the sword that pierced my heart.

Karen Garver Santorum

P.S. (14 years later): Our son, Gabriel, was a great blessing to our family and to families all over our country. Through his story, families were comforted and strengthened in their grief. In his life, we saw the goodness of God and the true meaning of unconditional love.

In 2008, Rick and I welcomed our eighth child into the world. Her name is Isabella Maria and we call her Bella, because it means "beautiful" and she *is* beautiful. Four days after Bella's birth we received the news that she has Trisomy, a serious genetic disorder similar to Down Syndrome only much more serious. We were told at the time that Trisomy 18 is a "lethal diagnosis" and that Bella's condition was "incompatible with life." We were told she would not live long—possibly a few days, a month at most. We have learned that type of toxic language frequently leads to lethal outcomes.

Bella is now almost four years old and we have celebrated her life every moment of every day. Bella is loved beyond measure, and she is very much at the heart of our family life. When we're playing board games or cooking in the kitchen, she's right there with us. She loves going for walks and playing piano with the other children. Bella smiles all the time and radiates a joy that will brighten any day. She is a very happy child.

"As they passed by he saw a man blind from birth. His disciples asked him, 'Rabbi, who sinned, this man or his parents, that he was born blind?' Jesus answered, 'Neither he nor his parents sinned; it is so the works of God might be made visible through him.'" (Jn 9: 1–3) Bella is an icon of God's face and filled with his love as he reveals himself through her and all people with disabilities. Bella is a teacher of unconditional love, and an education in the dignity of every person.

We think our sweet Bella is perfect, and we are honored that God chose us to be her family. Her life has a purpose, and she has taught us about what is more important in life. She completes our family and for her beautiful life we are eternally grateful!

IN LOVING MEMORY OF;

Gabriel Michael Santorum
October 11, 1996

*G*od needed an angel in Heaven
To stand at the Savior's feet;
His choice must be the rarest
A lily pure and sweet.

He gazed upon the mighty throng
Then stopped and picked the best,
Our child was His chosen one
With Jesus he's now at rest.

ANONYMOUS

${\mathcal{T}}$UESDAY, JUNE 25, 1996

If you remain in Me, and My words remain in you, ask
for whatever you want, and it will be done for you.
By this is my Father glorified, that you bear much fruit
and become my disciples.
(Jn. 15:7–8)

${\mathcal{M}}$y Dearest Baby,

Today is the day we learned I am expecting you. I wish you could see the joy and excitement this news brings to everyone—me, Daddy, your sister Elizabeth, and your brothers, Johnny and Daniel. I wish you could have seen us as we laughed and embraced upon learning the news—Daddy and I in the master bedroom, then your sister and brothers who had already been tucked into bed.

I like to imagine that somehow you did know of that initial joy and hope. A child is on the way! There is no greater news. You are going to change our lives, as every new baby does.

We quickly called our parents to tell them about you. Then later, in bed, I pulled out my prenatal books and read about what was happening to you at that very moment. And I realized, as I had in the past with your sister and brothers, that you are a miracle in so many ways.

I like to think that you have taken a place in our family this very evening. I like to think of you as a cause for laughter, celebration and hope. I like to think of the blessing of your life with-

15

in me on this day that God revealed you to us.

When we went to bed Daddy and I lay there wondering what else He would reveal to us through you. What kind of child will you be? What gifts will you bring? On this day, we can only guess and hope.

Good night, my littlest one.

Lord, You know we have desired this baby. Thank You for hearing our prayers. I pray You will bless this baby. Please help me to be the kind of mother You want me to be.

$\mathcal{S}$ATURDAY, JULY 6, 1996

The Lord is your guardian; the Lord is your shade at your
right hand. By day the sun cannot harm you, nor the
moon by night. The Lord will guard you from all evil,
will always guard your life. The Lord will guard your
coming and going both now
and forever.
(Ps. 123:5–8)

$\mathcal{I}$ want so much to be a good mother to you, even before you are born. That's why we are going to be watching you carefully as you grow.

Today was the day I had my first sonogram. It was your Uncle Jim, my own dear brother who also happens to be a talented obstetrician/geneticist, who did the sonogram for us. You have a family, little one—a family that waits with so much happiness for you. I had to have a sonogram early, because several years ago, when Elizabeth was eight months old, I had an ectopic pregnancy. Needless to say, it was a very difficult time for us emotionally, and we felt the loss. Now with every pregnancy the doctor needs to rule out this possibility. So we're here, all five of us, on this sunny clear day in New Castle, Pennsylvania, in Uncle Jim's lovely new office. We just want to make sure that you are where you should be.

Unfortunately, Uncle Jim cannot give us this reassurance; it's still too early to know. Life that is unseen and small, such as

17

yours, is a miracle and requires from us so much faith and trust. So much about you is still unknown, even exactly where you are inside me. I like to think that this is perhaps God's way of instilling in parents the patience and trust they will need to love and raise their chidren. Daddy and I pray this will be a healthy pregnancy. But already, we are surrendering you to God's care.

After the office visit, we went to the annual Garver family July 4th picnic in New Wilmington. Nothing is such a celebration of life as a huge family reunion, and our family has them all the time! It was the first time we've seen most of the family since discovering we were expecting you. The news was met with enormous excitement and joy.

It was a perfect day for a picnic—sunny, clear and warm. Elizabeth played on the swings and swam at the pool with the girls. Johnny joined the boys for games of hide and seek and pirate ship on the monkey bars. And little Daniel spent much of the day with Grandma and Granddad, either in the sandbox playing with his cars or going down the slide. When we left the picnic, your sister and brothers fell asleep the moment we put them in the car. A sign of a good day in a child's life.

While driving home I thought about how much I love being pregnant with you. I love your life within me. So many hopes and dreams are already focused on you. Be safe, be healthy.

Lord, I trust in You as the guardian of all things. I pray You will guide this baby safely into my womb where it can grow and develop under Your protection.

For this is our God, whose people we are,
God's well-tended flock.
(Ps. 95:7)

*D*addy and I pray every day that you have found a safe home within me.

Elizabeth also prays with her hands folded and in her sweet voice, "Dear God, please bless the baby in Mommy's tummy."

It's now part of the pregnancy routine with me. I have to get several blood tests over a series of days to determine if the hormone produced in pregnancy is rising normally. This is all part of ruling out an ectopic pregnancy. Fortunately, the numbers today are where they should be for this point in the pregnancy.

Dear Lord, I know that You are infinitely kind and loving. I trust in You as You tenderly watch over this new life inside me.

$\mathcal{M}$ONDAY, JULY 15, 1996

Children too are a gift from the Lord,
the fruit of the womb, a reward.
(Ps. 127:3)

$\mathcal{Y}$our sister and brothers were born surrounded by love and family. You will be born the same way.

Daddy and I want our babies to be born as they were delivered in years past with families present to share in the miracle. Your Uncle Jim delivered your sister and brothers, even though he wasn't my regular physician. Grandma and Granddad were also there with us and anxiously awaited the arrival of each new baby. Your Grandma remained right there in the birthing room through my laboring and deliveries, and, along with your Daddy, was a real source of support. We shared so much warmth and tenderness. Daddy and I were blessed to give birth to our children in this way.

During these years, we were living full time in Pittsburgh. But now we are starting to spend part of the year in Virginia, so we can all be together as a family as Daddy pursues his work in the Senate. I needed to find a new doctor in that area to look after me while we waited for your arrival. This was difficult for us because we had so much confidence in Uncle Jim and the two women in his practice. They are all very competent physicians.

The search for a new obstetrician took a while simply because our expectations list was so long. I finally found the person we were looking for in April of this year. Dr. Camilla Hersh is her

20

name, and she is extremely bright, board-certified, and very kind.

Anyway, that leads me to today when I had my first prenatal appointment which includes a lengthy medical history. One of the questions was if I wanted to have any prenatal testing done. In a way, the subject of prenatal testing goes to the heart of how we feel about our children, about bringing new life into the world. Your Daddy and I accept the life God sends us.

We made the decision about prenatal testing several years ago when Daddy and I were expecting your sister Elizabeth. On several occasions, we sat down to discuss prenatal testing with your Granddad, who is a brilliant pediatrician/geneticist. We were so fortunate to have his guidance. Granddad explained all the tests, including the accuracy, potential risks, and complications of each one. The alpha-feto-protein test just gives a mathematical probability that a baby may have a particular defect. It is not definitive and is a poor test because it causes so much anxiety in expectant parents. Frequently parents are led to believe something is wrong with their baby when everything is fine. The other tests, amniocentesis and chorionic villus biopsy sampling, provide definitive genetic results but are risky to the growing baby and could possibly cause miscarriage.

The decision was easy. We did not want to put our child's life at risk for the sake of our peace of mind, and if something were wrong with the baby, we would not consider abortion. So, it was years ago, that your Daddy and I decided against prenatal testing, except a routine sonogram, with our pregnancies. We had none for your sister and brothers, and we will not with you either.

Most importantly, we believe that you, Elizabeth, Johnny, and Daniel are miraculous gifts from God. Life is so precious. How do you

21

begin to decide on what terms you will accept to love and cherish a new life and on what terms you will not? Daddy and I are blessed with the lives of all our children—including yours. I could never say, I will accept and love a healthy baby, but not a sick one. Whomever God gives us, we will love and care for with complete devotion. My faith in God and my experiences as a nurse have reinforced this belief for me.

For several years I worked as a registered nurse in a neonatal intensive care unit caring for premature and sick infants. I frequently saw the initial anguish felt by parents after delivering a baby with a birth defect, and I lived through the pain with them. With time I also saw parents come to realize what a blessing their baby was and how that special child enriched their lives.

I will always remember a little girl named Rachel, who was born with anancephaly. Her parents were told during the pregnancy that because Rachel had no brain, nothing could be done to save her. I was present in the delivery room for her birth. Unlike the usual deliveries I attended, when the obstetrician handed little Rachel over to me, we did not rush to intubate and start intravenous lines; instead, we simply took her vital signs and kept her warm. For two days Rachel never left her parents' arms, and she died surrounded by the love of her family. I will never forget how touched I was by the love of Rachel's parents and so many others like them who unconditionally loved their infants in need.

Lord, You have blessed this family so much; with a strong and loving marriage dedicated to You and sweet, beautiful children who we know are gifts from You. Thank You for Your blessings, Lord.

*T*HURSDAY, JULY 18, 1996

He will love and bless and multiply you;
He will bless the fruit of your womb.
(Dt. 7:13)

I am now five weeks pregnant. Today Daddy and I saw your little heart beating and heard it on the sonogram machine!

It was the most beautiful sight!

Your little heart looked like a star twinkling in the night sky.

I could not take my eyes off you. It was so comforting to watch your heart beating and know you were safe inside me. You are your own little being through the miraculous genetic combining of all that makes up your father and all that makes up your mother.

The doctor could now make a definite diagnosis of an intrauterine pregnancy. You are right where you should be! I breathed a big sigh of relief and thought the most worrisome part of the pregnancy is over. Now I can enjoy a healthy pregnancy and look forward to the birth of a healthy baby.

Lord, thank You for blessing us with this beautiful new life safely home inside my womb.

WEDNESDAY, SEPTEMBER 4, 1996

Train up a child in the way he should go; even when he is
old, he will not swerve from it.
(Prv. 22:6)

I am now fourteen weeks pregnant. Getting through the hot summer months with Elizabeth, Johnny, and Daniel was a bit of a challenge since I was so tired and nauseated. But no matter how sick I got, it never bothered me too much because I knew it was all for you.

Throughout these past few months Daddy and I have thought about you every day. I am aware of your life within me continuously. I take a prenatal vitamin every morning, eat a healthy diet, exercise lightly, consume no alcohol, medicine, or caffeine, and I even stay away from the microwave oven and cellular phones! I want to do everything to make sure you are a healthy baby.

Daddy and I are so excited about the thought of having you, our fourth gift from God. We wonder what you are going to look like and what you will be like. In such heartfelt and intimate ways, we have bonded to you from the moment we knew of your existence.

Elizabeth and Johnny also share this attachment to you. They know there's a "little baby in Mommy's tummy." They frequently ask about you and want to know how big you are, if you're a boy or a girl, when they can hold you, and when you can come out to play! Johnny, who wants another brother, wants you to sleep in his room since Daniel is in the nursery. My precious baby, you will be so blessed having the most wonderful big sister and brothers.

Today, I had our second prenatal appointment. Everything went well. You are growing just the way the doctor wants.

Lord, I tell my children You have given us a most precious gift. Please help me to always speak of Your love and to follow Your examples so they may abide in You. Thank You for my children, Lord, for they are the light of my life.

*T*HURSDAY, SEPTEMBER 26, 1996

He was in the beginning with God. All things came to be
through him, and without him nothing came to be.
What came to be through him was life, and this life
was the light of the human race.
(Jn. 1:3)

*Y*our Daddy has been devoting his life lately to the debate on
partial birth abortion.* I know, it's hard to imagine there's anything to debate. There you are, my beautiful baby, in the silence
and peace of my womb. Daddy and I love you beyond words, and
we worry at times about the world you are about to enter.

Today, I got a chill down my spine as I sat in the playroom
reading to the children and watching the Senate debate on partial
birth abortion. I could not believe what I was hearing when a
Senator said: "No member of this Senate can face the trauma that
is represented by the issue of late-term abortion . . . . The men of
this Senate cannot be pregnant . . . . We are with this attempt to
override trying to substitute the judgment of a group of people who
do not have to go through this, who do not have to go through this
in life, or not have it even touch their lives."

A strange feeling came over me. True, we have never had a
child with a birth defect, but I am pregnant once again. We've had
no testing done, and we believe you're all right. Then I thought
about the sonogram scheduled for next week, and the what if's and
how awful it would be if you are not healthy. Tears filled my eyes,

and I placed my hands over you. For a moment I was troubled. I quickly put aside this most unsettling feeling and assured myself that you were perfect and healthy.

Elizabeth and Johnny looked at me and asked, "Mommy, why are you crying?" I smiled and told them I was fine and gave them each a hug and kiss.

Lord, I pray that You keep our little one in Your care. With Your help, Rick and I will do our best to change the world our children enter, making it closer to the way You wish it to be.

* A partial birth abortion is a procedure where "the doctor, using forceps, pulls the extremities (lower and upper), torso, and shoulders of the fetus through the cervix into the vagina. The fetus is oriented in a back or spine up position and its skull lodges in the internal cervical os (the opening into the uterus) because there is usually insufficient dilation for it to pass through. The doctor forces a pair of blunt scissors into the base of the skull creating a hole where a suction catheter is then inserted and the contents of the skull are removed through the catheter, followed by removal of the fetus." Stith-Coleman, Irene E. "Abortion Procedures," Congressional Research Service. The Library of Congress. 95-1101 SPR, Updated June 17, 1997.

Children, let us love not in word or speech
but in deed and truth.
(1 Jn. 3:18)

$\mathcal{D}$addy was home today. We spent the day with your brothers and sister working on puzzles, building castles, playing ball, and several children's games. In the evening, after reading bedtime stories and goodnight kisses, Daddy put his hands on my abdomen and said: "We love you, too, little one." Seeing this, Elizabeth and Johnny immediately put their hands over you and said, as they smiled: "We love you too, baby." And so it has gone for these many months. You are already part of our family.

We have your room all ready for you. It's right next to Daddy's and mine, and it's so cozy. It's done in rich blues and yellows with white furniture and bears on a picnic bedding and accessories. The walls are bordered with cute bears tucked in bed or reading books, flying kites, having tea, and taking baths.

You're going to love Elizabeth, Johnny, and Daniel. They have not just added a whole new dimension to our lives, but they have become the principle focus of our lives. They are each a complete joy! I love looking at their sweet faces and hugging them. I treasure every day with them. They share so many similarities and yet are so different.

Your sister Elizabeth is a beautiful child and has the prettiest

28

hair I've ever seen. It's curly, and springs up into ringlets all over her head when we brush it. She is a great big sister to Johnny and Daniel and, at just five years old, is very aware of you inside me. One of her favorite things to do is put baby Daniel on her lap and read to him. She reads well and likes to act out many of the stories complete with singing and dancing! She is so thoughtful, eager to learn, and very athletic. She will be a wonderful role model for you! Daddy built a little wooden playhouse for you children in the back yard and it's frequently *The Restaurant.* Together, Elizabeth and Johnny make grass spaghetti and blueberry mud pies! I'm sure she'll teach you how to make them! At prayer time we always ask God to bless our baby. Elizabeth always interrupts with "girl" after the word baby.

Johnny will turn four years old in November, and you'll love him as your big brother. He's a truly kind and gentle boy. He is so good with brother Daniel in sharing his trucks and teaching him how to build forts. He has beautiful green eyes and the most innocent expressions. Like Elizabeth, he, too, is very smart and learns things quickly. On our long trips back and forth from Pittsburgh to Washington, D.C., Johnny enjoys making up riddles and playing rhyming word games. He has a great sense of humor and likes to be a clown. He can't wait to teach you how to put puzzles together and build things. Johnny's now riding a big boy bike. I love to see the look of satisfaction on his face when he does well—he has a beautiful smile. By the way, he would love to have another little brother to play with.

Daniel is fifteen months old and cute as a button. He has big hazel eyes and a look that steals everyone's heart away. Like

29

Elizabeth and Johnny, he, too, frequently wants to curl up in a chair with Daddy or me and read stories. He enjoys finding things in the pictures. Daniel also loves sitting on our laps in the rocking chair with Daddy or me as we sing to him. His favorite rocking chair line is "Mommy, sing it again." He's especially interested in his toy cars and trucks, and he'll park them all in a line at the end of the day. Daniel looks forward to bubble bath time and is always the first one in the tub. He'll teach you how to make great bubble hats and beards! He isn't really aware of you at this point, but he loves babies—sometimes too much!

Your sister and brothers are so excited about you. On Thursday of this week Elizabeth and Johnny were having a quarrel and claimed they did not wish to be brother and sister anymore. I reminded them (as I often do), that as they grow up, no friendship is truer than those shared between brothers and sisters. Together they listened, and after cooling off a few minutes they apologized to each other. Later in the day, as if she had been thinking about it for a while, Elizabeth asked, "Mommy, will the baby inside you be one of my best friends too?" I was covered with flour because I was making an apple pie, but I wrapped her in my arms and assured her that, yes, you too, will be one of her best friends.

Dearest Lord, thank You for my children. Help me to love as You love. Please help me to be a mother who shows love, truth, and patience by living them. Instill Your spirit, Lord, into my children, and guide them with Your light.

TUESDAY, OCTOBER 1, 1996

You who dwell in the shelter of the Most High, who abide in the shadow of the Almighty, say to the Lord, My refuge and fortress, my God in whom I trust.
(Ps. 91:1–2)

I'm worried about you. You have been so silent and calm. In previous pregnancies I had always felt movement from as early as sixteen weeks. I'm now eighteen plus weeks, and have not yet felt you move within me. And I wonder if you're all right. On several occasions over the past two weeks, I have even taken the time to just sit quietly in the hopes of feeling you kick or turn over.

I expressed this concern to your Daddy, your grandparents, and the nurses at the doctor's office. They all assure me that everything's fine, that the pregnancy has not progressed far enough to feel you kick. I looked in my prenatal books, and they, too, say not to worry at this point.

But I have always felt that butterfly sensation with my previous pregnancies and have not yet felt even the slightest little kick or move from you. And there's something about a mother's instinct. Moms have a sixth sense about things—especially their children. It is troubling me that I fear something is wrong with you, little one. I have to know you're all right.

So I did something today that I have never done in a pregnancy. I acted like a frantic mom. In the morning when the doctor's office opened, I made an appointment to stop by so I could hear your heartbeat. When I arrived, I said to the staff, "I'm sorry to make your day busier, but I just have to hear the heartbeat." I did, and I was so comforted by the sound.

I called Daddy after the appointment. He laughed and thought I was a nut for worrying so much.

Lord, I place my life and the life of my baby into Your loving care. Father, I pray that You will bless and protect the baby growing inside of me. I pray that this child will be healthy, strong, wise, and close to You.

FRIDAY, OCTOBER 4, 1996

*Suddenly, a violent storm came up on the sea, so that the
boat was being swamped by waves; but he was asleep.
They came and woke him, saying, Lord, save us! We are
perishing!
(Mt. 9:24–25)*

If only this day could have ended as well as it began. Daddy
had taken the day off so he could be at the appointment I'd scheduled for a routine sonogram. We woke up to a warm sunny day,
had breakfast together with Elizabeth, Johnny, and Daniel, and
drove to the radiologist's office. We had been through this joyful
routine before. We were all happy and excited at the thought of
seeing you soon.

After sitting in the waiting area for a while, Elizabeth, who
was all smiles and full of excitement, looked at a woman sitting
across from us and proudly said she was going to see a picture of
the baby in Mommy's tummy soon. The woman smiled at me and
said she remembers how wonderful that was!

The test was initially performed by a sonographer who was
very quiet. In fact, she did not say a word. How strange. The
thought went through my mind that we were blessed to have my
brother do most of my previous sonograms. Uncle Jim told us
everything he was seeing and let us know immediately that everything was fine.

I lay there studying the screen. Daddy was also looking for

your little face, arms, and legs while trying to keep the children quiet. Everything seemed to be okay—head, spine, fingers, toes. But the sonographer kept going back to look at a black circle on the screen. I could not stand the silence anymore, so I asked what the circle was. The tech said it was the bladder. I assumed she meant mine.

The tech said she had to get the doctor, and before she left the room, Daddy and I asked her if everything was all right. She replied, "I'm sorry, but I'm not allowed to comment." Hearing this sent a chill through me. I had said those words before, while working as a registered nurse in the neonatal intensive care unit, but only when something was terribly wrong. Now I was overwhelmed with fear. Daddy stroked my head and, while kissing me, whispered: "It's all right honey, everything's going to be fine." I prayed my fear would be nothing.

A few minutes later she returned and said they had to move us to another room with a more sophisticated machine. Upon hearing this I worried about you. If they needed a better sonogram machine then there was something specific they were trying to see.

My heart began to race, and I started to cry. I then realized that the black circle could not have been my bladder. But then again, it could not have possibly been yours.

They kept us waiting for what seemed like an eternity. Then the doctor came in and drew a sword that pierced our hearts. With your sister and brothers present in the room and without the slightest trace of compassion or emotion, the radiologist studied the screen for a moment and said, "Your baby has a fatal defect and is going to die." Surely, he was missing something. He could not possibly be right with his diagnosis.

Several times the doctor said that you would die, and he repeatedly made reference to your fatal defect and the absence of amniotic fluid. You're a baby boy, and the physician said this defect usually occurs in male infants. When we asked him if there was any hope, he only shook his head, saying, "I have never heard of a baby live with this condition." He said I would either miscarry or deliver you at term, only to have you die shortly after birth.

I was sobbing. The thought of losing you was devastating. In one routine interlude of our lives, everything had fallen apart. The children were obviously upset. Their mommy was crying, and they wanted to know why. Question after question came pouring out of Elizabeth and Johnny. I tried to answer them but needed some time to pull things together. Your Daddy seemed to be holding up, so I asked him to take the children to the waiting room. As it turned out, he was one step ahead of me. He wanted to take the children out so he could settle them down and get to a phone. At this horrible time a name came into his mind that might give us some hope.

Through the tears emerged the most basic of parental emotions. We are not going to let you go. We decided that what this insensitive physician just told us was simply not true. You are not going to die, and we will go to the ends of the earth to save you.

Lord, here we are brokenhearted and wounded. Hear our cries for help. We have never known such great sorrow. We pray to You, Lord, to hear our prayers and answer our pleas for help.

Same day, after the office visit . . .

Save me, God, for the waters have reached my neck.
I have sunk into the mire of the deep, where there is no
foothold. I have gone down to the watery depths; the
flood overwhelms me. I am weary with crying out; my
throat is parched. My eyes have failed, looking for my God.
. . . I am afflicted and in pain;
let your saving help protect me God.
(Ps. 69:2–4,30)

Upon leaving the examining room I was taken to Daddy who was calling a Dr. N. Scott Adzick on the phone. Dr. Adzick is Surgeon-in-Chief of Pediatric Surgery at the Children's Hospital of Philadelphia. He also practices at the Pennsylvania Hospital in Philadelphia. Ironically, a few months earlier Daddy had visited Children's Hospital of Philadelphia as part of his duties as a U.S. Senator. There he was shown some of the advances they were making in medicine.

One person on the frontier of medicine working there was Dr. Adzick. He was pioneering surgery on babies not yet born. I remember your Daddy coming home that evening and telling me how impressed he was with Dr. Adzick as a human being and as a doctor performing amazing work with pediatric and intra-uterine surgery. Unable to reach him, Daddy left an urgent message.

After we left the office I cried uncontrollably in the car. I could not stop thinking of you and the sonogram image of your little body. You were in trouble and I had to make you well again—now. I retraced the steps of the pregnancy wondering what possibly could have caused this to happen. Was it the morning sickness? Was I eating well enough? Did I ever forget my prenatal vitamins? Did I stand too close to the microwave? What was it? What could possibly have caused this to happen?

I followed the doctors guidelines for a healthy pregnancy, and yet I felt responsible and angry at my body for not protecting you. I kept hearing the word fatal in my mind. I thought it so odd that this would happen following the partial birth abortion debate when reference was frequently made to babies with fatal defects. I loathe the use of the word fatal in reference to my precious baby. Say anomaly, say defect, say anything—but not fatal. All I can think is "God, give me a baby with a birth defect, any defect, and I will love and care for this child You have given me with total love and devotion—but, please God, please, don't take my baby!"

With this grief over the loss of a "normal" baby came a glimmer of hope. Dr. Adzick returned our call while we were driving home. He told Daddy it appeared as though you had "posterior urethral valve." Daddy repeated this to me in the car. When Daddy hung up the phone, he told me what Dr. Adzick explained. You have a valve in your urinary system that will not open. Because of this you are unable to empty the fluid from your bladder to the amniotic sac surrounding you, so there is no fluid around your little body.

Fortunately, Dr. Adzick told Daddy that he has seen and successfully treated babies with posterior urethral valve. He did add that the absence of amniotic fluid surrounding your body was not a good sign. But at least we have hope, and we hold onto this hope with everything we have.

37

After speaking to Dr. Adzick we called my parents. I am blessed to have for a father a nationally recognized expert in the application of genetics in the practice of medicine. My mother is the dearest and most giving woman I have ever known. Her entire life is devoted to her family. They were obviously extremely concerned about you and brokenhearted over the news. Granddad immediately began calling people to find out as much as he could. We called Uncle Jim and my sister, your Aunt Kathy, who is also a pediatrician. Granddad, Uncle Jim, and Aunt Kath were all able to provide us with more information about what is going on with you. We want to know everything possible.

While driving home Daddy also spoke with his parents, your Nanna and Pop Pop, and his brother, your Uncle Dan, about you. Uncle Dan was scheduled to come in for a visit with us this weekend with Aunt Missy and your cousin Caroline. As much as I love them, the last thing I want is company. I just want to go home and curl up in bed and cry for the next few days.

However, Daddy and I have arranged to see Dr. Adzick tomorrow morning in Philadelphia at the Pennsylvania Hospital, so having your aunt and uncle in town will be a great distraction for the children. In the end they were a godsend.

Lord, please heal our little one. Only You can touch our baby and make him well. We are on our knees begging You to please be with our child and us during this most difficult time.

Home after the sonogram . . .

*If I fly with the wings of dawn and alight beyond the sea,
Even there your hand will guide me, your right hand hold
me fast. (Ps. 139:9–10)*

I will never forget our arriving home and not being able to make it beyond the kitchen. Daddy and I were like two wounded birds. Daddy, barely able to stand, bent over with his head in his hands and wept. I sat at the table weeping with my head in my folded arms.

Our lives were spinning out of control. There you were — beautiful you—cradled inside my womb—warm and nourished and loved. And yet, you were in trouble. I felt so helpless. I did not have the power to make everything right. Daddy and I desperately prayed to God to touch you and make you well.

Soon Daddy and I pulled ourselves together and sat down with Elizabeth, Johnny, and Daniel on the couch. We explained what had unfolded during the day. We said: "When someone you love is sick it makes you sad. We are crying because the baby in Mommy is sick, and we do not know if we can make him better."

Johnny asked, "Mommy, are you sad the way you get sad when I'm sick? Then Elizabeth said, "Mommy, when we're sick, you and Daddy always make us better. You can make the baby better too." Daddy and I did our best to provide comfort to the children. We gave them lots of hugs and tried to inform them in a way they would understand.

We had a long talk with Grandma and Granddad after our talk with the children. Their love and support helped strengthen us. Your grandparents notified all your aunts and uncles and their families, and everyone began to pray for you. Daddy and I called his parents, our closest friends, and the priests at our church to start offering up prayers on your behalf. In one of the calls, someone said, "Well, get ready to let go." It crushed us to hear this. It's not within the nature of parents to give up hope for a sick child—especially when you've just received the painful news.

In our conversations with Father Jerome Fasano and Father VanderWoude from our church, they encouraged us to trust in God. They said that God permits things to happen at times for a greater good, that God does not will evil things, only good things. They said God gave us this gift of life to care for, and this is our opportunity to love our child. Father VanderWoude said: "God always forgives, men sometimes forgive, but nature never forgives." He went on to explain that since God is loving and forgiving, He doesn't use times such as these as punishments. Rather, God created our child in a special way for a reason. This conversation strengthened Daddy and me, and it reminded us of the importance of faith.

I will never forget the visit today from Dr. Lloyd Ogilvie, the Chaplain of the Senate. Daddy has become very close to Lloyd partly because of a weekly Bible study they attend with several other Senators. Daddy called Lloyd when we got home to ask him to pass the news on to our friends in the Senate so they could keep us in their prayers. Daddy is fortunate to have so many friends in the Senate who are Christian brothers. When Daddy got off the phone he told me Lloyd was coming here. I asked if Lloyd was aware that we lived twenty-five miles from the Capitol and it was rush hour. Your Daddy said he told him that, but he's coming.

When Lloyd arrived, we hugged and we cried. I asked, "Why us? Why now?" It was not lost on any of us the coincidence that, one week after the debate in the Senate on partial birth abortion, we were being confronted with a pregnancy not unlike the cases used to defend that procedure.

Lloyd told us to trust in God. He told us to pray for God's guidance, and He will give it to us so that no matter what happens, it will be what is the best for us and our son.

I pressed for more: Was God doing this to our son to test us? Was this because we had not, as one of the Senators said on the floor, ever had to face a pregnancy gone awry? What was God doing to us? Lloyd reminded us of God's assurance in Hebrews 13:5, "I will never leave you nor forsake you." He helped us claim again that you are a gift from God and that He would not test us with your sickness. Lloyd said, "God does not cause sickness or send it as a punishment. He has allowed us to live our lives in a world in which sickness does exist."

Lloyd went on with empathy to say, "God is the healing power of the world. He uses doctors and medical science, but He is the Healer. He wants healing, wholeness for us, but sometimes that wholeness is to be realized in heaven. The child in your womb, Karen, is a sacred life, a child of God. Your son will live forever in heaven, no matter how long he lives here on earth. Now you must trust God completely, commit your fears and

41

anguish to Him, and allow Him to give you supernatural strength and courage to know that He will work out everything for His glory and your son's ultimate good."

We put our arms around each other as Lloyd prayed for God to fill up the diminished wells of our hearts with His Spirit so that, with the gift of faith, we could place you in His strong and capable hands.

Daddy and I live by the motto, "Life is about being there." Never was this so clear as it was today by Lloyd's being there for us.

Later, in the evening, Aunt Missy, Uncle Dan, and Caroline arrived. It was so hard not to fall apart. Everything we talked about seemed so unimportant. The only thing on my mind was you—you completely consumed my every thought. All night long Daddy and I lay awake in bed holding each other, holding you—until the sun lit the sky.

Lord, we are feeling so much pain and anguish, and it feels like You are so far away. Please help us not to despair, but rather to find strength in knowing that no matter where we are or what we are going through, You are always here with us. Please bring us Your calm and abiding peace to strengthen us during this time.

Saturday, October 5, 1996

You are my God; pity me, Lord; to you I call all the day ...
Lord, hear my prayer; listen to my cry for help. In this
time of trouble I call, for you will answer me.
(Ps. 86:3, 6–7)

Daddy and I, along with your brother Daniel, left first thing in the morning for Philadelphia. Aunt Missy and Uncle Dan stayed at our home to watch Elizabeth and Johnny.

Daddy and I prayed the rosary out loud together for you. In fact, we prayed the entire trip to Philadelphia. We asked God to heal you and make you well. It was hard believing this was real, and there was a part of me that actually thought this was just a bad nightmare.

The three-hour drive to Philadelphia seemed to last forever. Dark gray clouds covered the sky as the rain fell through the cold morning air. How appropriate for the sun to be hiding at this somber time. The humming of the car engine never sounded so loud. All the cars traveling beside us seemed to be moving in slow motion.

We arrived at the Pennsylvania Hospital, and we met Dr. Adzick in the obstetrical unit. His demeanor was gentle and humble. He spoke with an enormous sense of concern and compassion regarding our situation. While he was obviously a brilliant man, he spoke in terms that we could understand.

Daddy's friend, Rob Bickhart, met us at the hospital and played with Daniel during the testing. Having five children, Rob knew just what to do. They looked through children's magazines, colored, and walked through the lobby and cafeteria.

Shortly after our arrival to the hospital, we began the sonogram. This was done under the direction of Dr. Alan Donnenfeld who specializes in perinatology. The most important thing they needed to do during this test was a thorough evaluation of your kidneys. Dr. Adzick and Dr. Donnenfeld watched the sonogram screen closely for a long time. The sonographer took all sorts of measurements from many different angles.

Daddy and I were able to watch everything on a monitor as it was happening. We were kept informed on every move and what it meant for us. They again said that the absence of amniotic fluid was not a good sign. It meant there was a complete obstruction. We were told this was the most rare, most severe, and most often fatal form of post urethral valve syndrome. In addition, your kidneys—under pressure due to the bladder not emptying—were "dense and bright." This meant they were probably not functioning. Daddy and I went to Philadelphia hoping for some glimmer of hope to hold onto. We were given none.

Originally we had gone to the hospital planning to have the sonogram and hopefully a bladder tap performed. Now, because of the "brightness" of your little kidneys, we have to rethink the bladder tap. It is an invasive procedure where a long needle is inserted through my abdomen into your bladder to remove the fluid inside for testing. We do not want to interrupt your quiet and peaceful life within me unless we think it is necessary to save your life. My womb shields and protects you, and I have reservations about subjecting you to invasive observation and treatment.

Please be with us, Lord. Guide us through this time, and instruct us with what it is You want us to do.

Still Saturday ~ After the sonogram . . .

...Dare the clay say to its modeler, "What are you doing?"
or, "What you are making has no hands?"
Woe to him who asks a father,
"What are you begetting?" or a woman,
"What are you giving birth to?"
Thus says the Lord, the holy One of Israel, his maker: You
question me about my children, or prescribe the work of my
hands for me! It was I who made the earth and created
mankind upon it; It was my hands that stretched out the
heavens; I gave the order to all their host.
(Is. 45:9–12)

$\mathcal{D}$addy and I began discussing our situation with the doctors in the sonogram room and then moved to a room across the hall that provided chairs and a quiet place to talk. The neonatologist from the N.I.C.U. joined us. So there we were: three physicians, Daddy and I, and you. We were sitting in this room because of one minia-ture valve, smaller than a pinhead, that is not working and will ulti-mately kill you if we do not intervene—one tiny valve!

The doctors said, in most of these cases, there is no other accompanying defect. The way Dr. Adzick put it was, "The baby's genetic make up is like a blueprint for a house. In this case the blue print is perfect, but one of the parts installed isn't working like it was designed." I was so upset—one tiny valve that is not opening is going to cause you to die! I felt so frustrated with my body for not protecting you and so angry at that valve for not working correctly. Then I thought about the Psalm in the Bible that

45

reads, "You formed my inmost being; you knit me in my mother's womb" (Ps.139:13). I had to remind myself that we are not the ones in control here on earth. Only God is, and His hand is upon us now, little one. The Creator of all life is knitting you together, forming you with more love and skill that either Daddy or I could ever imagine. "Have faith, Karen" was all I could think through much of this.

I wanted to cry, but I had to hold myself together so we could intelligently discuss our options. This seemed impossible, but I managed to put my emotions aside for the moment. Dr. Adzick and Dr. Donnenfeld explained everything. You have "obstructive uropathy associated with posterior urethral valves" which usually only affects male babies. Most amniotic fluid that surrounds a baby in utero is made up of urine. Since you are not able to empty your little bladder, there is an absence of amniotic fluid which the doctors referred to as "oligohydramnios."

The physicians explained that this is extremely serious, because amniotic fluid not only cushions you, but more importantly, it is essential for your lung development. If we do not do anything, you will die at birth from severe "pulmonary hypoplasia" or undeveloped lungs that will not allow you to breathe. Also, since your bladder will not empty, it is putting pressure on your internal organs and causing damage with every part of you. The doctors went on to say that what you have—posterior urethral valves associated with oligohydramnios—has a 100 percent mortality rate. I then thought about that insensitive physician the day before. He was right.

Dr. Donnenfeld then said that he was obligated to provide us with all our available options. He said he knew we would not be interested in the first one, but legally, he had to mention it. He said,

"Your first option is to terminate the pregnancy." As soon as the word pregnancy left his lips, the lights went off in the room! The neonatologist quickly got up and turned the lights back on—they were on a timer. We all nervously laughed, and Daddy said, "I guess that answers your question."

We love you, little one, more than words can express, and we don't want to lose you. We would go to the ends of the earth for you. Never for a moment did the thought of an abortion even enter my mind as an "option." It seems about as appropriate an option as a physician telling us that we could terminate the life of our six-year-old child if he or she were diagnosed with stage four leukemia. It doesn't make any sense to me as a mother to make distinctions that really do not exist. You are no less of a child to us than Elizabeth, Johnny, and Daniel. Confronted with this defect of yours, your Daddy and I will make every attempt to love, care for, and cherish you until the end of your own natural life. It is our role as parents to do everything we possibly can to help you, Elizabeth, Johnny, and Daniel through all difficult times—all throughout your lives—and this certainly includes your life inside me right now.

It's our nature as your parents to want to protect you. It is impossible to understand God's infinite mind. I'm so confused and filled with anguish, but what I do know is that I must be strong and not lose my faith in God. He knows what He's doing. God said that He would instruct and teach us in the way we should go, that He would counsel us with His eyes upon us. God, who is always present in our lives, will provide us with direction.

The doctors told us that the next option was to do nothing and let you die—which was definitely no option. And last, Dr. Adzick explained that we could start by doing two bladder taps, one today and one tomorrow, to determine kidney function. If your kidneys were working, which given what we knew was not likely, a catheter shunt could be placed by sonographic guidance into your little bladder to allow your urine to drain directly into the amniotic sac, thereby bypassing the obstruction. Dr. Adzick said that survival after catheter placement in babies like you was about seventy percent. Assuming all goes well after you are born, Dr. Adzick could then surgically repair the malfunctioning valve.

And there it is! That glimmer of hope—that glimmer of light in a dark storm that we had so desperately been looking for! This means the world to us.

Dr. Adzick referred to this procedure as "in-utero decompression," because it would relieve your tiny organs from the pressure of your bladder and restore amniotic fluid. Dr. Adzick did stress that you were about to go through a critical time with the development of your lungs. We needed to provide you with amniotic fluid so your lungs would have room to expand and grow. He said, "The earliest possible intervention will provide the best prognosis."

Daddy and I asked the physicians for their opinions, since medically they had dealt with other cases like this. Were we being too extreme in wanting to go ahead with the testing? Then Dr. Adzick said in his very calm way, "If you were my wife, I would want to do the tests." This was so helpful to Daddy and me, because it reaffirmed in us our decision to do everything to try and save you. I can understand why some physicians use non-directive counseling, but at times like this, it can leave patients with uncertainty when they have difficult decisions to make. We will always remain grateful to Dr. Adzick for giving us his personal opinion.

48

After our decision to treat your problem, we returned to the sonogram room for the initial bladder tap. By this time it was late morning. Dr. Donnenfeld did the procedure under sonographic guidance, while Dr. Adzick remained there with us providing medical information and emotional support.

I had so much anxiety before the test at the thought of interrupting the peace you have within my womb. It seems wrong to pierce the womb that protects you and keeps you safe. But then, not doing the procedures means giving up all hope and allowing your death without any attempts to save you. To protect you at this point means trying to correct the complications associated with your defect.

Daddy held my hand and we prayed silently all through the bladder tap as we anxiously watched the sonogram screen. It hurt, but how I felt did not matter. What worried me was you and how you were feeling. We could see the tip of the needle entering your bladder, and we prayed that God would make it painless for you.

You did well, but Dr. Donnenfeld was concerned when he saw the urine he withdrew for the sampling. It was clear, and this is not a good sign for kidney function. So, another letdown. Before Daddy, Daniel, and I left the hospital, Dr. Donnenfeld informed us they would call with the results later in the day.

Lord, we cannot possibly face this time alone. We need You. For it is You Lord who gives us courage. Please turn our weakness to strength and our despair into hope.

Later that day ~ Saturday, October 5, 1996 . . .

I raise my eyes toward the mountains. From where will my
help come? My help comes from the Lord, the maker of
heaven and earth. . . . The Lord is your guardian; the Lord
is your shade at your right hand. By day the sun cannot
harm you, nor the moon by night. The Lord will guard
you from all evil, will always guard your life. The Lord
will guard your coming and going both now and forever.
(Ps. 121:1–2, 5–8)

During our long trip back home we prayed and cried a lot. It was then we decided to name you. And we knew we had to give you a name that suggested a pillar of strength. After much thought and discussion about how God sends angels into people's lives when they need protection, Daddy and I decided to name you after the two great Archangels. Your name will be either "Gabriel Michael" or "Michael Gabriel." Gabriel means "Strength of God". He was God's messenger, and he comforted Jesus in His agony. Michael was the strong and youthful angel who stood guard over God's people. The name Michael means "Who is like God." The two names are perfect for you.

Daddy and I prayed that you would be under the watchful care of the great Archangels. We prayed that Archangel Gabriel would comfort all of us in these trials and sufferings and give us God's strength. Daddy and I recalled how the Archangel Gabriel appeared to Mary saying, "Do not be afraid, Mary, you have found favor with God." Imagine how distraught she must have been—unwed and

50

pregnant! How beautiful Mary's answer: "Be it done unto me according to Thy word" (Lk. 1:20–33). Mary trusted in God's word, and so must your Daddy and I. We must place our lives and your life into God's hands, and He will take care.

Shortly after we returned home your Uncle Dan and Aunt Missy drove in with your brother, sister, and cousin. They had been to a farm for a fall festival. We were bombarded with stories of the wonderful time they had—hay rides, face painting, farm animals, and lots of apples and apple cider. Each person was permitted to take a little pumpkin home. They were especially proud of the two smallest ones they got for Daniel and for you.

Late in the afternoon, Dr. Donnenfeld called with the results of the bladder tap. Unfortunately, they were poor and indicated that your kidneys are not filtering out impurities. Another sword pierced our hearts. We asked him about doing the second bladder tap and if there was much chance of the results changing. Dr. Donnenfeld said it was unlikely the results would change that much, if at all. These results were not even close to the normal range of kidney function. In order for them to be able to proceed with a bladder shunt, a miraculous improvement would be necessary. However, Dr. Adzick was insistent about going ahead with the second bladder tap as scheduled. His reason was that the urine collected today was "stale," and the tap tomorrow would test urine recently made by the kidneys.

Dr. Donnenfeld tried to prepare us for the worst. He described our situation as "grim." He said, given the visual condition of your kidneys and this test result, he would expect that the kidneys have stopped functioning. He warned that your kidneys are probably not producing urine and that we should not be sur-

51

prised if there was no fluid in your bladder tomorrow morning.

I got off the phone with only one thing on my mind: We had to get your little kidneys working. Prayer! We had to reach as many people as we could and ask them to pray for your little kidneys. Daddy and I called our family, friends, and clergy to update them and ask them to focus their prayers on getting your kidneys to work. I don't know how good a prayer or how many prayers it takes for God to grant a miracle, but I was determined to have both quality and quantity on our side.

Daddy and I went to the 5:30 P.M. mass at St. Catherine's of Siena, which is the church we attend when we are at our Virginia home. It was there that I felt you move for the first time! It was the most beautiful feeling, and I smiled and began to cry right there in church. It felt so wonderful feeling your little arms and legs moving around as if you were playing. You moved around a lot. I put Daddy's hand over you, and you kicked hard enough for him to feel it several times! We will never forget that moment.

After church we spent the entire evening praying and reading through articles on your condition. We are trying so hard to understand what is going on with you while sifting through all of the medical information. We spent so much time discussing all the details, risks, complications, benefits, and success rates surrounding the possible surgery. We carefully weighed the pros and cons of each side amid so much stress and with so little time. How unfair that in the midst of this tragedy we even have to make such a decision.

That evening Daddy and I came up with an idea. We thought that if I drank a lot of water, maybe you would have more fluid in your system too, and thereby produce more urine. I drank what seemed like gallons of water that night. I had to do something. In the end I knew that our best hope was to give it up to the Lord and pray for His intervention —and we did all night long.

God, please help us to know that You are here with us always, and You understand our fears. God, we place all our worries and fears in Your hands, and pray for grace and strength during this time. Please continue to guard our lives.

$\mathcal{S}$UNDAY, OCTOBER 6, 1996

Ask and it will be given to you; seek and you will find;
knock and the door will be opened to you. For everyone
who asks, receives; and the one who seeks, finds; and to the
one who knocks, the door will be opened.
(Mt. 7:7–8)

$\mathcal{M}$y Dearest Gabriel,

The alarm rang. Had I even fallen asleep? It was 4:15 A.M.

I wanted so much to sleep, so you could get your strength back. Daddy said we had to get up now, we can't be late—not today.

I lay in bed afraid. Afraid that today would be the last day to hope.

On the drive up, little was said. Yes, we were both tired, but each of us was focused in prayer on your little kidneys. They had to be working by now. They just had to be.

Daddy and I arrived with your brother Daniel at the Pennsylvania Hospital in Philadelphia at 7:50 A.M. Rob again took Daniel for us, and together they explored the hospital. Dr. Adzick was there once again to help us through what promised to be a dark day. While not overly optimistic, he was ever hopeful, and this meant a great deal to us.

Daddy and I anxiously awaited the picture of you on the sonogram screen. The first thing we desperately looked for was fluid in your little bladder. After a few minutes of searching, Daddy called out, "There it is—there's fluid in his bladder!" Joy, more importantly hope! We could continue on.

Dr. Donnenfeld put the needle through me as before, but this time it didn't seem to hurt as much. In the end he was not able to obtain much fluid. We hoped there was enough to run the test. Again, Dr. Adzick was there with us providing strength and comfort. He was cautiously optimistic and told us of a few cases where babies like you had surprised everyone and survived. He said that miracles do happen—and we believe they do. *Thank you God, for being with our little one; please touch Gabriel's little kidneys and make him well.*

On the way home we talked again about your name. We decided to call you Gabriel Michael, in that order. We did not put the Michael first because it's too popular. We wanted you to have an obviously holy and sacred name. So my beautiful son, you now have a name, and we pray to the Archangel Gabriel to comfort us in our agony, and ask Michael to protect you from all harm. In the coming weeks and months, we expect these two names will come to have enormous significance.

When we returned home, Uncle Dan and Aunt Missy were on their way to take the children to the circus. Their visit was really a blessing. The children had a wonderful time all weekend, and the activity kept their attention away from their two tired and distraught parents. Daniel, who has been traveling with us, has been remarkably good—not just good for a one-and-a-half-year-old, but good period.

Daddy went along to the circus to have some time with the children. I stayed home and waited for Dr. Donnenfeld's call. Finally, late in the afternoon, the phone rang, and Dr. Donnenfeld was on the other end saying, "Are you sitting down?" I went to sit on my bed for fear that I would not be able to bear whatever he was about to tell me. He went on to say, "I can't believe this. I've never seen anything like this. Karen, the results are not just good—they're great!"

Finally I could cry tears of joy! Dr. Donnenfeld went through all of the specifics of the lab results, and it was so wonderful hearing his happiness and relief. He said he's never seen such a dramatic change from one day to the next. A miracle had occurred, for according to the laws of nature, good test results were impossible and could not be medically explained! Gabriel, your kidneys are working!!! They're working!!! Sing praises to God!!!

Daddy soon called, and he, too, cried happy tears. Gabriel, you now have a chance of living, and because your kidney function is so good, hopefully there will be fewer complications.

We spoke at length with Dr. Adzick later in the day. He was thrilled with the results. He arranged to have Dr. Bud Weiner perform the shunt procedure. Dr. Weiner had done this procedure more than any other physician on the east coast and had invented a catheter for it. During these past few days, Dr. Adzick has been so helpful explaining everything to your Daddy and me. He's been so patient and kind while we've asked him hundreds of questions. He faxed us several articles and sent more in the mail. We want to know everything about what is going on with you. In our conversation today he explained what to expect in the procedure and answered many more questions for us.

Dr. Adzick explained that a multidisciplinary team would manage and care for you. Gabriel, you are now under the care of many physicians who are very concerned about you. They will take the best care of you, and we thank God that Dr. Adzick and his team are close in Philadelphia. Later in the day Dr. Bud Weiner called us to explain in detail the procedure, its risks, and possible complications. He informed us that this is a procedure we will probably have to go through a few times, since intra-uterine catheters usually only last several weeks and then fall out. He has been successful with the procedure and was confident all would go well. He did add that it was important for you to have fluid in your bladder. We scheduled the intra-uterine surgery for Tuesday, October 8th. *God, please bless us with your spirit of peace; comfort us and protect our baby.*

During these past few days we have kept Elizabeth and Johnny informed in very simple ways about what's going on with you. They are worried about you and know you need some help. Since Uncle Dan and his family have left for home, our task is now more of a challenge. Tonight we gave the children a lot of extra hugs and kisses. They are grieving too, and we think it's important to include them and to provide loving comfort to their little hearts and minds.

After tucking Elizabeth in tonight, she looked at me and said, "Mommy, is Gabriel going to die?" I couldn't hold back the tears. We held each other, and I assured her that we were going to do everything to make you better, but that I did not know what God had planned. I said: "We pray our little one will be fine, but if Gabriel is called by God to come to heaven, he will be in such a beautiful and happy place—happier than we could ever imagine." Elizabeth smiled and said, "Mommy, if Gabriel goes to heaven, can I go up there to see him?" All I could do was smile at the sweetness of her question and say, "Hopefully, we will all be there together someday."

Gabriel Michael, I hope you feel how loved you are. Can you hear us when we talk with you? Can you hear us when we sing you songs? And do you feel our hands when we place them over you? We are all so concerned and worried for you, but we believe you are going to make it. We are praying for you and your little kidneys.

Lord, encouraged by Your infallible words I ask You to have pity on us and pray You will heal our little Gabriel.

Monday, October 7, 1996

Cast all your worries upon Him because He cares for you.
(1 Pt. 5:7)

I spent the day making plans for tomorrow. I arranged for a baby-sitter to be home with Elizabeth, Johnny, and Daniel. There were meals to make, train reservations to be booked, and laundry to clean. Daddy was working, and it was best we were both so busy. Although no matter what I was doing or who I was talking with, you were on my mind continuously.

At one point in the day, when I went up to the nursery to get Daniel a toy, I sat motionless in the rocking chair looking into the crib, wondering if you will ever lie in it. I wish I knew that everything is going to be all right. I want someone to assure me that this will be your soft bed where Daddy and I will tuck you in, cover you with warm blankets, and watch you sleep. I need someone to tell me that I will be able to sit in this chair and nurse you as I sing you lullabies. But there is no person who can assure me of anything right now. It's so difficult living with this fear over you.

As much as I've read, I feel frustrated that I don't know more. There's not a lot of literature on your condition or much experience doing surgery. Dr. Weiner is the expert on the procedure we are about to have. He has done more than any physician on the east coast, but there have only been a dozen or so. All of these unknowns leave me feeling so unsettled. Gabriel, I'm so worried about the surgery tomorrow. I pray you will do well, and

I can tolerate the pain. I hope the procedure itself goes smoothly and without complications.

When Daddy returned home in the evening we prayed together as a family for you, Gabriel, and the surgery tomorrow. When we pray the children always include their own prayers expressing what's on their minds. Elizabeth and Johnny prayed, "Dear God, please take care of our little brother. He is a special boy, and we love him so much."

Lord, I place all of my worries and concerns before You now and pray for peace. I know that You care about all of us. We ask for Your protection.

$\mathcal{T}$UESDAY, OCTOBER 8, 1996

*For God commands the angels to guard you in all your
ways. With their hands they shall support you,
lest you strike your foot against a stone.
(Ps. 91:11–12)*

$\mathcal{I}$ could not sleep at all during the night. Worry for you consumed my every thought. I read passages in the Bible searching
for strength. Then I came upon this one and focused on it for the
rest of the night, *"Oh God, you are my God ~ for you I long!
For you my body yearns; for you my soul thirsts, Like a land
parched, lifeless, and without water. So I look to you in the
sanctuary to see your power and glory. For your love is better than life; my lips offer you worship!" (Ps. 63:1–4)*

Daddy and I arrived at the Pennsylvania Hospital at 11:30
A.M. The surgery was not scheduled until 12:30 P.M. This gave us
some time to sit in the waiting area on the obstetrical floor and talk
with God. The catheter shunt would be inserted into you through a
metal tube. The tube looked huge, but in reality it was only big
enough to allow Dr. Weiner room to work the long probe with the
catheter at the end. Dr. Weiner would have to make an incision in
my abdomen to insert the tube. I was told it would be painful,
because they could not administer the local anesthetic deep inside
me. Just the thought of this was making me feel as though I might
faint. I had to keep telling myself not to think of the details, but to
focus on God and you, Gabriel—who I would do anything in the

world for. *Oh God, Daddy and I need You today. We are so concerned about little Gabriel, and pray that he will be safe during the procedure. He's just a little over nineteen weeks ~ so small and fragile ~ he needs you, Almighty God. Please watch over our little one. I am so afraid about the procedure today. Please be with me, and give me the courage to endure any physical pain.*

Soon the medical staff were all there—Dr. Adzick, Dr. Donnenfeld, Dr. Weiner, and three registered nurses. The time your Daddy and I had wished for had come—the procedure that would save your life. I felt so sick and afraid but knew that for you, my little one, I had to have courage to go through with it. "God give me courage" was all I could think over and over again in my mind. I wanted to be a pillar of strength for you, Gabriel, and by focusing on you and my prayers I had a degree of courage that I never thought was possible. If saving your life means we need to go through this procedure twenty times, then I'll gladly do it.

The procedure began, as usual, with a sonogram. Fortunately, there was fluid in your bladder but, to our dismay, not as much as anticipated. We had waited two days so that your bladder would be full, thus a bigger, easier target for the shunt.

So we were faced with another decision. This procedure at your age was difficult enough to perform with a full bladder, but with such a small target, we questioned whether or not Dr. Weiner should do the surgery or if we should just put it off another day or so. The physicians all decided that waiting during this critical time in your lung development would not be wise. After all there was no guarantee your bladder would fill. In the end, as difficult as it would now be, Dr. Weiner felt confident about the outcome, so we decided to go ahead with the procedure.

Daddy held my hand, caressed my face, and he said comforting words to me all throughout the surgery. I concentrated on other things to minimize the pain. I prayed to God for strength of mind and body for both of us, Gabriel. A few times I watched the screen to see you, and to make sure you were all right. As Dr. Weiner performed the procedure, he worried about me because I was so silent. He said, "Say something to me. Are you all right?" I explained that I was fine, and had to focus on other things in order to get through this.

The surgery took longer than expected. At one point Daddy even suggested that we come back tomorrow and try again. But at this point all of the doctors said to continue. Dr. Weiner persevered and amazingly placed the tip of the catheter in your tiny bladder with it draining into the amniotic sac surrounding you. The procedure was done! You did well, and I remained still on the table, did not get sick, and tolerated the pain. *Thank you, dear God ~ the catheter is in place!*

The only complication was the time it took to place the shunt. Dr. Weiner did a superb job, but it took almost twice as long as normal to perform the procedure. This meant twice as much time for bacteria to enter into my womb. The risk of infection under normal circumstances was about one in 200, but for us now it is higher.

I was able to walk slowly and carefully after the procedure. Daddy and I met in a conference room with Dr. Weiner, Dr. Adzick, and his wonderfully supportive registered nurse assistant, Lori Howell. There they gave me post-op instructions and answered a lot of questions. Like any surgery, their greatest immediate concern was infection. They emphasized that if I had any abnormal cramping or a temperature of 100 degrees or above, to notify them immediately.

They went on to say that if I developed an infection in my uterus, this would be extremely dangerous, even a life-threatening situation. I asked if I would be given antibiotics to protect you, but the physicians said antibiotics could create a major health risk by actually masking the signs of an infection within the womb. Dr. Adzick said that antibiotics would not sufficiently enter the amniotic sac to prevent infection. I was a little confused by this and did not want to think about the possibility of getting an infection. I know we'll be fine, Gabriel. I'll take it easy, follow the doctors' orders, and we will get through this.

Before leaving, Daddy and I asked the physicians if I could take the trip to Pittsburgh, Pennsylvania, we had planned. They said it would be fine as long as we delayed it a day so I could rest. All your aunts and uncles, your Daddy, and I have planned a big celebration for Grandma and Granddad's fiftieth wedding anniversary. Daddy and I seriously considered not going, but since the doctors gave the okay, we thought it would be fine.

Actually, going to Pittsburgh means I will have a lot of help from my family with the care of your sister and brothers. I am blessed to be in an extremely close family so full of love and support.

We're delaying the trip a full day while I rest.

God, thank You for keeping Gabriel safe. We pray for Your protection. Thank You for creating the angels most splendidly who carefully watch over us. Please take especially good care of our little Gabriel. Keep him safe and healthy.

*𝒯*HURSDAY, OCTOBER 10, 1996

You formed my inmost being; you knit me in my mother's womb. . . . Your eyes foresaw my actions; in your book all are written down; my days were shaped, before one came to be. (Ps. 139:13,16)

I prayed for this child, and the Lord granted my request. Now I, in turn, give him to the Lord. (1 Samuel 1:26–27)

*𝒜*fter resting all day we drove into Pittsburgh late Wednesday evening. Daddy took care of everyone, as he always does. He did all the cooking, laundry, and packing when he returned from work so I could rest. On the way to Pittsburgh Daddy and I spoke about how you would be in medical journals someday for surviving a major anomaly. You could be a light and hope to other desperate parents going through this same situation.

We arrived late at night, unpacked, said our prayers, and went right to bed. But I could not sleep. I was awake from 3:00 A.M. and on through the long night. No matter how hard I tried, I could not fall asleep. I prayed, I relaxed my body, I tried many different positions, but nothing helped. I rested, but sleep did not come over me. I was not feeling well—nothing specific, just uncomfortable.

Then the cramps started at about seven in the morning, after Daddy had left for work. I thought maybe I had eaten something that had given me indigestion. Or perhaps the cramps were because I was full of anxiety at not being able to fall asleep. I've delivered three babies, and I know what labor contractions feel like; this did not seem like labor. During all of this, I was worried about you, Gabriel, and I prayed to God to watch over you. We had come this far, and I could not possibly be getting sick. I figured it was the long drive the evening before and the lack of sleep. I stayed in bed trying to rest.

Thank God my mother was there with me. She is truly an angel, and the best Mom in the world. The children adore their Grandma, and she helped me with their morning care.

By 8:30 A.M. I was feeling worse, as if I had the flu with chills. My temperature was 100.5 degrees, and it was then that I panicked. I was so afraid. I knew I had to call the doctor but did not at first. I checked my temperature again and again and again. It kept reading 100.5 degrees! I started to cry. Maybe the thermoscan was not working right. So my mother got a regular thermometer and this read 101 degrees! I began weeping. This could not possibly be happening!

As I lay there on Grandma and Granddad's couch, the chills worsened, the cramps grew more intense, and my fever remained. I sobbed uncontrollably. Grandma said, "Honey it can't be as bad as you think—you're not going to lose little Gabriel." I told my Mother that they would want to deliver you. Dr. Adzick and Dr. Weiner had explained that if I got an infection in my womb, it's a life threatening situation for both of us, and the only way to treat it is through delivery. I couldn't bear the thought of that.

By about 10:15 A.M., realizing I could wait no more, I pulled myself together, with the help of my mother, long enough to contact the physician. Dr. Donnenfeld was really down when he heard the news, and sighed saying in a soft voice, "Oh, that's bad—that's really bad." He then instructed me to go to the hospital and see Dr. Alan Hogge, an obstetrician/geneticist, because his group specializes in high risk pregnancies. He said he would call the doctors with the details.

I was crying on the phone. The sword had pierced through my heart again. After having the catheter placed, Daddy and I were confident that things would be fine, and you would go down in medical history as a baby who survived posterior urethral valve. This was not supposed to be happening! You are not going to die!

I called Daddy's scheduler, Aunt Nancy, to whom I'm very close, and told her the news. She, too, became extremely upset and began to cry. Aunt Nancy immediately contacted your Daddy on a car phone. Daddy was on his way up to Erie, Pennsylvania, on Interstate 79. His driver, Tony Fratto, made a U-turn and immediately they headed back to Pittsburgh. Daddy called me right away to let me know he was on his way. He said everything would be all right, but his voice cracked as he said it. Aunt Nancy also called Granddad, who was at a breakfast, and Granddad came home.

I began to pray that I had pneumonia, or a kidney infection or the flu—give me anything—but not little Gabriel!

Daddy flew through the front door to take me to the hospital. He told me that he had called Monsignor Bill Kerr, our dear friend who is President of LaRoche College north of Pittsburgh. As busy as he was, Monsignor Kerr insisted upon meeting us at the hospital. I so wanted him there, but it made me worry even more about what awaited us at the hospital. The entire trip to the hospital I prayed that I had something that would make me feel this poorly. Daddy bundled me in blankets and held me in the back seat. Granddad sat up front while Tony drove. They talked about what was happening, but for me it was background noise. I was in my own world trying to hold it together and stay focused on a fading glimmer of hope.

Lord, please let there be something wrong with me—not little Gabriel. Please let these signs of sickness either pass or be an infection in me that is treatable. Lord, please protect my precious baby.

At the hospital ~ Thursday, October 10, 1996 . . .

My God, My God, why have you abandoned me? Why so
far from my call for help, from my cries of anguish? My
God, I call by day, but you do not answer; by night, but I
have no relief. (Ps. 22:2–3)

*T*he hospital staff were waiting for us in the labor and delivery
unit. All I could think about was how I did not want to be in the
"labor and delivery" unit. Did this mean they had given up hope
for you before even seeing us? You are not going to be delivered
today! You are just twenty weeks! You are not ready to come out!

We were immediately taken to a room where they checked
my blood pressure, heart rate, and temperature, then put me on a
fetal monitor. It was almost noon now, and my temperature continued to climb to over 103 degrees. The cramps had turned into
painful contractions.

I couldn't stop shaking. It was so cold.

Heated blankets! They were warm at first, but that didn't last
long. More heated blankets! It was so cold.

The obstetricians, Dr. Cynthia Simms and Dr. Susan Ponkey,
kept asking me questions about how I felt. They were concerned,
because if it was an infection in my uterus (which they called
"chorioamnionitis") there was a danger that I may go into shock
and die.

Tests and more tests. As tedious as it was, I felt as long as
they were testing, there was still hope that they would find something wrong with me that would not jeopardize you. Then came

the worst test of the day. Dr. Watt-Morse did the sonogram that broke our hearts.

Your Daddy stared at the monitor, and I stared at his face. He smiled. Then I saw his tears. "It worked, honey. The surgery worked." I turned my head to see you surrounded by amniotic fluid. So much that, for the first time, we saw your arms and legs moving! You finally had room to move. The shunt was working perfectly, the surgery was successful, it had worked like a charm—but it was all to no avail. How cruel an irony. Either way, Gabriel, we lose. I couldn't take my eyes off you. You were so cute. You looked so healthy. We had prayed, we had fasted—why was this happening?

My contractions were increasing in strength and intensity, and my temperature was almost 105 degrees. Even with ten blankets on, I was so cold. There were conversations going on around me, but I couldn't focus on them. The world seemed to be fading in and out. All I could think of was that beautiful baby on the sonogram.

Your Daddy held my hand and said Dr. Simms had something to say to me. Dr. Simms, Daddy, Monsignor Kerr, and Granddad all gathered around me. Looking at their faces, I knew. I guess I knew all along, but there was no doubt now. I wanted to close my eyes to shut them out or jump out of the bed and run away from this nightmare. Dr. Simms calmly and kindly explained that the source of infection raging within my body was the amniotic sac. The only way to treat this was through delivery. Dr. Simms went on to say when the amniotic sac was removed, I would be fine.

I would be fine! But what about my baby? What about Gabriel?

Dr. Simms said, "There is no way to treat an intra-uterine infection. . . . I'm so sorry . . . . there's nothing we can do." These were the most difficult words Daddy and I have ever had to come to terms with. This couldn't be! Through the tears I kept saying— "Please, don't tell me there's nothing you can do! There must be something you can do, something, anything, somewhere in the world. I'll do anything if it means saving Gabriel!" Dr. Simms, who appeared so grieved and frustrated at not having the ability to save you, only said, "I'm so sorry. I wish there was something we could do."

Dr. Simms went on to say that you would have to be delivered soon. She said we needed to start high doses of antibiotics to protect my life, but warned that even though I would begin to feel better, the infection was continuing to worsen. The antibiotics would not enter the amniotic sac in sufficient amounts to treat the infection. In addition to administering high doses of antibiotics, she also wanted to start a medicine called pitocin to "help move the labor along."

Hearing this made me cry harder. If your time in me, Gabriel, is limited, and God is calling you home to be with Him, then I want you to remain here in your home within me for as long as possible. I can't bear the thought of losing you—and I wasn't going to give up hope. I agreed to having the antibiotics but not the pitocin.

Having worked as a neonatal intensive care nurse for several years I knew that at just twenty weeks gestation, you would not even be sent to the neonatal intensive care unit, Gabriel. I begged them to stop the labor, but Dr. Simms said that to do so would be malpractice, and I would die from septic shock.

Daddy began calling our doctors in Philadelphia desperately begging them for help. He spoke with Dr. Donnenfeld and Dr. Weiner. They were both so kind, so caring, but they, too, had run out of options. I lay there in bed thinking about how we have the technology to send astronauts and satellites into the far reaches of the universe with unfailing precision, and we have the most sophisticated medical technology available right here in this country—microscopic brain surgery, laser surgery, gene manipulation techniques, fetal surgery in utero. And they can't treat my infection!

Your Granddad and Monsignor Kerr provided so much comfort during this time. Granddad helped us to understand what was going on medically and provided love and emotional support. Monsignor Kerr was a spiritual pillar of strength. It meant so much having him there to pray with and to reassure us that letting go of you, Gabriel, was the right and moral thing to do. Monsignor told us to place our trust in God. In his very calm voice, he said we had done all we could to save you. That it was time to hand you over to God who was calling you home. He assured us that you would soon be in a better place, knowing love we cannot begin to understand.

The antibiotics were starting to work. My temperature was coming down and I was lucid again. Daddy got on the phone with our "fountain of hope," Dr. Adzick. Surely he would know of something we could do. But Daddy eventually handed me the phone. I asked hoping . . . . . well, just hoping. Dr. Adzick's

72

voice was filled with such sorrow. I felt his grief for you. I thanked him for all he had done for us.

In tears, I handed the phone back to your Daddy. He, too, thanked Dr. Adzick and hung up the phone. It was finally over. I will never forget the look on your Daddy's face, as he hung up the phone. He looked at me shaking his head. Then he held his head in his hands and sobbed.

At around 3:30 p.m. the nurses who had been working during the day were leaving. I'll never forget one sweet nurse who took care of me. She had been so dear through all this. When she came in to say good-bye she expressed only sorrow and said she wished she could do more to help us. Then she broke down. For a few precious seconds she hugged me, and we cried together.

Since I had been crying all day, the doctor asked the nurse to give me something to help me sleep. I had kept my hands placed over you all day, Gabriel, talking with you, praying for you, and trying to capture every fraction of a second that we would share together. So, as tired as I was, sleep was the furthest thing from my mind, because I felt like I would miss some precious time with you inside me. But I was completely exhausted, and every bit of me ached. The nurse gave me something to help me calm down and sleep.

I am so confused, Lord. I place all of my concerns for my baby before You. I know that You love both me and little Gabriel. As I sleep I know You will watch over us and protect us.

Late Afternoon ~ October 10, 1996 . . .

You will grieve, but your grief will become joy.
When a woman is in labor, she is in anguish because her
hour has arrived; but when she has given birth to a child,
she no longer remembers the pain because of her joy that a
child has been born into the world. So you also are now in
anguish. But I will see you again, and your hearts will
rejoice, and no one will take your joy away from you.
(Jn. 16:20–22)

I awoke to the love and comfort of my mother, who had been
sitting at my bedside for a while holding my hand. It was so good
to see her, and having her there meant so much to your Daddy and
me. She has more love in her than anyone I've ever known, and I
have always been so blessed having her in my life. Grandma lost
four babies and knows the heartache we were feeling.

I also awoke to painful contractions. These fierce contractions made me realize that, in fact, God was calling you home.
Why He was calling you home so soon puzzled me greatly. At
this point, the only thing Daddy and I could do was accept His
will for you. But I could not say "Thy will be done." I was still
so desperately holding onto you, Gabriel, hoping and praying
for a miracle. I couldn't let go of you.

My contractions continued to progress. They were just as
painful as my three previous labors. But unlike my three previous labors where the pain had a beautiful purpose and was soon
forgotten with the sound of a crying baby, the pain with you was

magnified tenfold by the thought that the contractions would end in silence. I have never known such great pain.

Lord, help me to give up my pain to You. I need You, and trust in You as You prepare me for the birth of this precious child.

Evening ~ October 10, 1996 . . .

Jesus, however, called the children to himself and said, "Let the children come to me and do not prevent them; for the kingdom of God belongs to such as these".
(Lk. 18:16)

See that you do not despise one of these little ones, for I say to you that their angels in heaven always look upon the face of my Heavenly Father.
(Mt. 18:10)

*A*ll through the day, I had been asked what seemed like hundreds of times if I would allow them to give me the pitocin. I said no every time because I could not bear the thought of pushing you out of me any sooner than you were already naturally coming.

Eventually, however, the physicians became extremely concerned, and so did your Daddy. He was worried that if we did not move things along he may lose me. He cried and spoke to me softly, saying, "Honey, you've been in labor all day—you've done everything possible to save little Gabriel—it's just a matter of time now. What about our marriage? I can't live without you. What about Elizabeth, Johnny, and Daniel? They can't live without their mother. Karen, you make our lives complete—please, it's time—I love you so much."

It was all such a nightmare that brought with it the darkest night. I was lost in my anguish and couldn't see ahead of me. What consumed my every thought was the precious little time I

76

had left with you, Gabriel, and how my three other precious children at home also need me. I love all of you so much, and this grief has left me so confused. I did not want to talk with anyone—no more doctors, nurses and experts. Instead, I just wanted to be alone with you. Even after every expert in the hospital spoke with me about the final diagnosis and the severity of it, I still could not bring myself to believe the truth. Surely a miracle was going to happen and you were going to surprise everyone. Then I would deliver you at term, and you would be fine.

As we got later into the evening, the physicians became more concerned that I would go into septic shock. Daddy whispered in my ear as tears poured down his face: "Honey, your body is not forcing Gabriel out of you—Gabriel is leaving us to go and be with God—with God, Karen." Indeed, my labor continued to progress, and I began to come to terms with the inevitable—you were going to come whether I liked it or not. God was indeed calling you home. *"Be it done unto me according to Thy word."* I now realized that no matter what I did, I was completely powerless in the face of God. He's the one in control. God needs you, Gabriel, and I need to be here to love and care for Elizabeth, Johnny, Daniel, and your Daddy.

Oh God, help me to leave little Gabriel to Your mercy, as You left Your son to our mercy. Help me to offer You the life of my child ~ who is really Your child. Please dear God, fill me with peace in knowing that Gabriel will soon be safe in Your arms. Keep me focused on Your heavenly Providence and help me to acquiesce to Your will.

*I urge you therefore, brothers, by the mercies of God, to
offer your bodies as a living sacrifice, holy and pleasing to
God, your spiritual worship. Do not conform yourself to
this age but be transformed by the renewal of your mind,
that you may discern what is the will of God.*
(Rom. 12:1–2)

*Most admirable and worthy of everlasting remembrance
was the mother, who saw her seven sons perish in a single
day, yet bore it courageously because of her hope in the
Lord. . . .[she said] these words: "I do not know how you
came into existence in my womb; it was not I who gave you
the breath of life, nor was it I who set in order the elements
of which each of you is composed. Therefore, since it is the
Creator of the universe who shapes each man's beginning, as
he brings about the origin of everything, he, in his mercy,
will give you back both breath and life".*
(2 Mc. 7:20–23)

Gabriel, I pray that I will trust in the Will of God, and keep my
heart and mind fixed on the important tasks now before us. We
have come on this journey together, you and I as one. I have loved
the oneness that has connected us. I weep at the thought of having
to surrender it.

But now we have reached the painful reality of our situation,
and we must physically part. Your Daddy and I often talk about

how difficult it will be someday to let our children go to have their own lives and independence. For you, my little one, I did not think this "letting go" would come so soon. It seems so unfair that you should die without ever having the chance to live a full life.

I am already missing you, Gabriel. Losing you will be a profound loss, and I can't begin to express the immense heartache your Daddy and I are feeling. We wished for you and prayed for you even before you existed. Daddy and I were looking forward to welcoming you into the world, hearing your first cry, seeing your first smile, and feeling your first tender kiss. We imagined how special it would be to sing you lullabies, rock you, hold you, teach you your first words, watch you take your first steps. We are so deeply going to miss the chance to see you grow through the years. No one will ever take your place in our lives and in our hearts. So now, I pray that God will give me the strength to release you with peace and grace as you enter into your spiritual journey with Him.

Dr. Daniel Edelstone came in to check me again at about 12:40 A.M. You were born at 12:45 A.M. It was a silent birth. How I would have loved to have heard a cry, loved to have looked into your beautiful eyes.

It was important to us for you to be baptized, and Daddy baptized you as soon as you were delivered. You were alive!!! You were pink and warm and beautiful, and we could see your little heart beating in your chest. That beautiful sign of your life will change us forever.

Though your eyes did not open, they allowed us to see in you the face of God. While you did not give a cry, you spoke so powerfully to our hearts. You lay there in our arms so tenderly and yet so full of strength. You were a child of courage and love. You may not have been perfect in the eyes of the world, but you were perfect in our eyes and in the eyes of God.

Daddy and I bundled you in a blanket and put a hat on your head to keep you warm. We held you ever so close, sang to you, spoke softly in your perfect little ears, and held your perfect little hands and feet. We could not stop kissing and hugging you. We took many pictures and made little hand and foot prints onto paper. As sad as it was, the time with you gave us a chance to love and care for you. There you were, our beautiful son, your life so brief, and yet, your impact so great.

I thank God with all my heart in having blessed us with some time with you. Gabriel, you lived for two whole hours after your birth, and at 2:45 A.M. you went to your home in heaven with God.

*A*nd I heard a cry

That of a mother weeping
For the child
that was no more

And the wail echoed
across the mountain peaks
of her agony

And it sounded
down the years
it seemed
to all eternity

It was a cry
of such utterable pain
and grief
from a mother's
shattered heart . . .

From "At The Death of a Child"
by DONALD L. DEFFNER

Lord, I cannot begin to understand why You had to take little Gabriel. It hurts more than words can say. But what I do know is that You have a plan for everything, and everything is for Your Glory. Please help me, Lord, to keep my faith in You during this extremely difficult time.

81

Morning ~ Friday, October 11, 1996 . . .

*Thus says the Lord: In Ramah is heard the sound of
moaning, of bitter weeping! Rachel mourns her children,
she refuses to be consoled because her children are no more.
Thus says the Lord: Cease your cries of mourning, wipe
the tears from your eyes. The sorrow you have shown
shall have its reward, says the Lord .
(Jer. 31:15–16)*

*In all circumstances give thanks, for this is the will of
God for you in Christ Jesus.
(2 Thes. 5:18)*

*Y*ou had a peaceful death. Daddy was holding you when you left
us. We thank God for the two hours we had with you, for it meant the
world to us. It is a beautiful thought that in your whole life you only
knew love and kindness. You have escaped the pain and temptations
of this earthly existence. I now think of you as so very fortunate.
Daddy and I always say that our most important role as parents is to get
our children into heaven, and now we have one there in you.

Normal procedure at the hospital is to transfer anyone who dies
into the morgue. Just hearing the word "morgue" in reference to you
put a chill down my back. Daddy and I made it clear to the nurse that
in no way were you going to go "to the morgue." I couldn't allow my
baby to be put into a dark refrigerated room! Gabriel, you were going
to remain in our arms until we had to part with you at your grave.

We kept you bundled and slept with you in our room during the
night. In the morning, your Grandma, Granddad, Aunt Maureen, Aunt
Sis, and Monsignor Kerr all came to visit. They all held you and loved
you. We cannot begin to put into words what their visits meant. They
provided so much comfort.

The funeral director called in the early morning and asked when we wanted someone to pick you up. Again, we couldn't bear the thought of handing you over to strangers, kind as they were. Daddy and I wanted to hold you for as long as we possibly could. Kirk Freyvogel, the funeral director at Freyvogel's in Pittsburgh, was so kind and empathetic. They helped us handle the details with your funeral mass and burial.

The first call we received after your death early in the morning was from our friend Cardinal Anthony Bevilacqua in Philadelphia. After expressing his deepest and heartfelt condolences, he told us something that has provided so much comfort and strength. His Eminence said, "Your baby is in heaven, he is now a saint—don't pray for Gabriel—pray to him to intercede on your behalf with our Heavenly Father." We have a saint living in the face of God! How beautiful!

There were many papers to sign before leaving the hospital. In them you were described as a "twenty-week-old fetus!" I was so upset to see this! You were not a "fetus," you were our baby, fully formed and beautiful, just like a full term newborn, only smaller. The nurse apologized and accommodated my wishes by changing all of the descriptions of you to "twenty-week-old baby."

Daddy and I left the hospital with you in our arms, and your Aunt Sis and Monsignor Kerr again at our sides. Grandma and Granddad were home watching your siblings, and we arrived at Grandma and Granddad's early in the afternoon. After much discussion, Daddy and I decided that since we had kept Elizabeth and Johnny informed all along, we should allow them to hold you. We were a little concerned about what their reactions might be, but since they were grieving, too, we thought it would be awful for them never to have held or seen you.

83

Your siblings could not have been more excited about you! Elizabeth and Johnny both held you with so much love and tenderness. Elizabeth proudly announced to everyone as she cuddled you: "This is my baby brother, Gabriel; he is an angel." Elizabeth and Johnny adored you and thought you were "the cutest baby in the whole world!" They whispered sweet things in your ears, and sang you lullabies. Elizabeth wanted to change your clothes and get you dressed up for your Mass of the Angels. I told her that we had to keep you warm and bundled. Daddy and I took several pictures of you with Elizabeth, Johnny, and Daniel. Including them was a good decision. It helped them feel a part of two very important family events—your birth and death —and it brought a finality to the fact that you were no longer in me.

We spent the entire afternoon in Grandma and Granddad's living room with you in our arms. We talked with you about so many things. One of the most important things that I now realize is that you have not left us, but rather you remain—and always will remain—here with us. Gabriel, because of you, Daddy and I are now elevated to another dimension of our lives. We have entered into the spiritual realm with you, my son, now living in the face of God. As your mother, I so desperately have and will continue to grieve the loss of our earthly journey together; but we are now on an infinite spiritual journey.

Lord, why You had to take little Gabriel is beyond my understanding. Even though I may weep, it is not without hope. I know You have a plan for my little one. Thank You for choosing my son to be a part of Your divine work. Thank You also, Lord, for blessing Rick and me with some time to love and care for our beautiful baby.

Early evening ~ Friday, October 11, 1996 . . .

*Jesus answered, "Amen, amen, I say to you, no one can
enter the kingdom of God without being born of water and
Spirit. What is born of flesh is flesh and what is born of
Spirit is spirit. Do not be amazed that I told you, You
must be born from above". (Jn. 3:5–7)*

*M*onsignor William Kerr brought out the spiritual significance of your life during our Mass of the Angels. We had the Mass
in Grandma and Granddad's living room at 4:30 P.M. We made a
beautiful altar with a handmade lace tablecloth that your Great
Grandmother Weisburg made years ago. Your tiny casket was
placed upon a small table that was also adorned with lace and a
white linen cloth. We placed a beautiful basket of flowers which
we received from our friends, Linda and Don Nickles (Don is a
Senator from Oklahoma), at the foot of the table. It was a simple,
yet moving service reflecting the simplicity and power of your life.
My brothers and sisters were all there. Your Daddy's Aunt Stella
was also there with us. Grandma and Granddad's living room was
filled with only love for you, Gabriel.

After Mass everyone knelt down to say a prayer and good-bye.
After everyone had left the room, Daddy, Elizabeth, Johnny, Daniel,
and I were alone with you once again. Elizabeth and Johnny helped
as we arranged your little casket nicely with a blanket, a blessed cross,
and a small soft toy that Daddy bought at the hospital for you. We also
put a family picture in with you. Elizabeth, Johnny, and Daniel then
kissed the little hat on your head and said their good-byes.

Daddy spent a few minutes holding you and saying good-bye, and he gently placed you into my arms. This was the last time I would hold you and kiss you, the last chance for me to bundle you and keep you warm, the last time I could whisper in your ear and hold your little hands. This was the last chance I had to mother you in the way I am so deeply going to miss. It was too much to endure. I sat on the living room couch, holding you tightly against me as I wept, and could not let you go.

After a while of patiently waiting, the funeral directors came in and asked if we were ready. I asked, "Can I please have just one more minute?" I had made several more "one more minute" requests when Daddy realized I really needed some help. With Daddy's love and support I was able to hand you over to Monsignor Kerr who then placed you into your little casket. After they closed the casket, I opened it to take one last look at you. Seeing you lying there wearing your little blue handknit hat and sweater made all of this seem as if it were not real. There will never be another you, Gabriel.

We placed your casket on the back seat of our van, and I sat beside you as we drove to the cemetery. It was a quiet drive. The family stood closely together at your grave. Monsignor Kerr led us in prayer, and once again blessed your casket and the ground where you were to be placed. You'll be next to my brother—your Uncle Johnny—who died eight months after his birth. You are also next to your great grandparents and great-great grandparents. We know they'll look after you.

After the groundskeeper lowered your casket into the ground and covered it with dirt, the children sprinkled your grave with the flowers that Don and Linda Nickles gave us—daffodils, lilies, iris, and lilacs. They were colorful, and filled with sweet innocence, like you.

Lord, You know how difficult it was for us to leave Gabriel's grave. He was a part of our family, and now we must leave him behind. I have to keep reminding myself that Gabriel is still with us and always will be. He is so fortunate to have been born into a new and beautiful life with You. Please help me, Lord, to remember Your promise of everlasting life when I so desperately want to hold Gabriel in my arms.

Saturday, October 12, 1996

Your word is a lamp for my feet, a light for my path. . . .
I am very much afflicted, Lord; give me life
in accord with your word.
(Ps. 119:105,107)

Today is your Grandma and Granddad's fiftieth wedding anniversary. I am so happy for them, because they truly have a marriage made in heaven. Except for your Daddy and me, I have never seen two people so in love!

My siblings and I have always been richly blessed in having a mother and father who always loved and cared for each other and their children more than anything in the world. Grandma and Granddad are our role models in our marriages and in our parenting. Their strong bonds of marriage united them in a lasting and loving relationship which made for the family closeness and security we have always known. I thank God everyday for my dear parents, and I hope He continues to bless them with happiness, health and many more splendid years together.

Gabriel, I have been looking forward to this day for so long. We have all sorts of special surprises planned for the party, including the unveiling of a most extraordinary handmade picture quilt we have been working on for months. I was so excited for this day—until we lost you. And now I'm not sure if I have the strength to go.

I just want to stay in bed for the next few days and cry. I don't want to get dressed, I don't want to have to smile, I don't want to have to eat, I don't want to have to talk with anyone, I don't want to do anything that will take me away from my thoughts of you. The thought of going to a party the day after your death is too much. I've been awake crying all night, and I ache all over. I feel so empty and numb—and I'm desperately longing for you. I can't possibly go out today—and I can't imagine how things can continue on when the world has come to an end.

I especially cannot go to a celebration, and on top of that have a family picture taken. But then again, Gabriel, it's my parents' fiftieth. For fifty years their lives have been joined in a sacred union. Together they have walked through life, celebrated births, worked hard to raise a family, shared their dreams, enjoyed the happy times, and comforted each other during life's trials. Fifty years, and they are still so in love—and they are still so affectionate with one another. I pray your Daddy and I have as good a marriage.

Grandma, Granddad, and the entire family have been so excited about this day for at least a year now. If we are not there we will be missed. I look at my parents and I see only love, patience, and kindness. They will never have another fiftieth. Gabriel, I cannot miss their big day, and I pray that you will be there to comfort your Daddy and me during it.

God, I pray that You will give me the strength to get through this day. It's going to be difficult not crying and falling apart. I am feeling unbearable pain, and I miss Gabriel so much. Please, dear God, help me to give up my pain and sadness to You for today, so my parents will have a wonderful fiftieth wedding anniversary.

$\mathcal{S}$UNDAY, OCTOBER 13, 1996

There is an appointed time for everything, and a time for
every affair under the heavens. . . A time to weep, and a
time to laugh; a time to mourn, and a time to dance.
(Eccl. 3:1,4)

$\mathcal{T}$he anniversary mass was lovely and full of grace, especially when Grandma and Granddad renewed their marriage vows. After mass, everyone went to Churchill Valley Country Club for a family picture, social hour, and lunch. Daddy and I were exhausted and not up for socializing. Instead we went to your grave with some flowers. We know you are with us always, Gabriel, but we had this overwhelming need to be where your little body is laid. The multi-colored leaves on the hillside were lovely in the sunlight. We sat on the ground as we prayed and talked to you surrounded by the beautiful dying leaves of autumn.

We returned in time for the family picture. Somehow I managed a smile. I'll never look at that picture without thinking of you.

I did not want to sadden this special day for my parents. We wanted them to enjoy their day. It was hard to believe there were any tears left, but every time I thought of you they were there waiting to spill out. I had to concentrate on not falling apart. But my family was there—as they always are—comforting and supporting us.

Grandma and Granddad had a beautiful day, and I
thank You, Lord that we were there for it. Thank You Lord,
for making us realize that this day was far too important to
miss. Thank You for giving us the strength to get through the
day. We're so happy we were there to share such a special day
with two of the most special people in our life.

*M*ONDAY, OCTOBER 14, 1996

Those who sow in tears will reap with cries of joy. Those
who go forth weeping, carrying sacks of seed, Will return
with cries of joy, carrying their bundled sheaves.
(Ps. 126:5–6)

*W*e're back home now. Away from the love and support of
my family. It was so difficult leaving them—and especially
you—back in Pittsburgh. I was awake all night thinking of you in
that cold, dark grave. It seems so wrong. You should be warm
inside me.

I think I'm losing my mind. I feel kicks inside me that aren't
there. When I move in certain ways I'm still careful—like I was
when you were inside me—and have to remind myself that you're
no longer there. I called your brother Daniel "Gabriel" today. I
keep pulling out your pictures to look at you and holding your
blanket as if to feel a part of you. Out of habit I've taken my prenatal vitamins each morning since you left, and today this made
me break down and cry. I put the bottle away in your keepsake
box as I was once again reminded of the piercing emptiness of
your loss. I keep begging God to put you back into me. I keep
asking, if He raised Lazarus from the dead, then why can't He put
you back in my womb! It's all such a terrible nightmare. How I
wish I could wake up and realize it was all a bad dream. I am
numb, exhausted, and depressed.

My milk let down today. When I realized what had happened I cried hysterically. How could God do this? Haven't we been through enough! I nursed all of my babies, without bottles, for at least a year. Nursing my babies was so important to me. They all nursed well, and are healthy and secure because of it. To me nursing is one of the most beautiful things a mother can share with her child. I loved nursing! And now my breasts are full of milk that was made for you, that you will never know. This is without a doubt another dagger through my heart. It's the final insult.

Lord, please help me to see that it is during these difficult times that You are strengthening and shaping me. Please comfort me in my troubles, and please help me to keep any anger from entering my heart.

*T*UESDAY, OCTOBER 15, 1996

Learn from the way the wild flowers grow. They do not work or spin. . . If God so clothes the grass of the field, which grows today and is thrown into the oven tomorrow, will he not much more provide for you. . . seek first the kingdom [of God] and his righteousness . . .
Do not worry about tomorrow;
tomorrow will take care of itself.
(Mt. 6:27–34)

*O*ur home is filled with the sweet scent of flowers, especially pretty baskets of wild flowers, my favorites. There are plants everywhere. Never have I realized how much flowers and plants—living things—mean to people who have lost a loved one. Somehow I feel your breath of life is present in these flowers.

We received hundreds of sympathy cards yesterday and today. Daddy and I read them together. They were filled with such heartfelt outpourings of emotion for us, Gabriel. Reading them was like therapy, and it helped us a great deal. The most moving cards were those written by parents who had also lost babies, and were sharing their stories.

I have spoken to my parents and my siblings often since leaving Pittsburgh. I usually talk to your Grandma and Granddad every day, but now we are talking a few times each day. They know the immense heartache we're feeling. We have spent hours talking about what happened, what might have been, and how to

93

survive the death of a baby. Grandma and Granddad have helped Daddy and me so much.

Your Daddy's parents, Nanna and PopPop, sent a beautiful letter today. It was filled with sorrow and questions about us losing you and how we need an enormous amount of faith at times like these. We were so touched by the letter, because at the end they acknowledged your life, little Gabriel, in a very special way with a gift to remember you by. This really meant so much to us.

Gabriel, people have sent cards and meals and flowers and baskets of everything you can imagine. And I am so grateful to them. But I am so sad because all I want is you.

Lord, I know that You are here, and are comforting me. Please help me always to be aware of Your presence in my life and all the things You do to care for me and my family.

# WEDNESDAY, OCTOBER 16, 1996

Do not let your hearts be troubled. You have faith in God;
Have faith also in me.
(Jn. 14:1)

Just as you Know not how the breath of life fashions the
human frame in the mother's womb, So you know not the
work of God which he is accomplishing in the universe.
(Eccl. 11:5)

*T*oday as I was grocery shopping with the children I saw a pregnant woman who looked as if she were due any day. I wished I were still pregnant with you. Then the thought went through my mind that maybe we should not have had the surgery. Perhaps the outcome would have been better if we had not intervened at all. Needless to say, this was a very unsettling feeling. I had to remind myself that God is the one in control, and He has a plan for you, Gabriel.

You will always be our special and cherished son. No one will ever take your place in our hearts or in our family. Your sweet face is sketched indelibly in my mind. We miss you so much but know that someday we will be reunited with you in heaven.

The timing of this has left us extremely puzzled. We had three previous pregnancies that were perfectly healthy, giving us beautiful babies. Gabriel, you were hopefully not going to be our last child. Why didn't this happen with an earlier or later pregnancy? Why did it have to be a fatal defect? Why did it have to happen at all? This is an issue that your Daddy and I will struggle with for a long time. And we believe it was no coincidence that this occurred at the same time as the partial birth abortion debate on the U.S. Senate floor. A debate that your Daddy led. God was at work here, Gabriel, wasn't He?

Daddy worked tirelessly with his colleagues in an attempt to override President Clinton's veto which eliminated the ban on this brutal procedure. During the debate there was a continual reference to babies who had various fatal birth defects. As I mentioned in an earlier letter, two Senators who support partial birth abortion implied that your Daddy had no right to speak on this issue because "he has never given birth," and the "men of this Senate . . . are . . . people who do not have to go through this, who do not have to go through this in life, or not have it even touch their lives."

Gabriel, your Daddy and I did not just "go through this"; we agonized and suffered more than words can express. This did not just "touch" our lives—it forever changed them. Will your Daddy's arguments be more authentic and believable and persuasive now that he's "been there?" Did God do this to make your Daddy's arguments more powerful when the debate comes up again? I do not know why you were taken so soon. I can only say what I believe in my heart as your mother. I do know that God has a reason for taking you so soon.

Just as Saint Gabriel was the great Archangel whom God specially appointed to bear some of the most important biblical messages, I believe, through your life, your Daddy and I will be inspired to deliver a message. We pray that Saint Gabriel and you will help your Daddy as he tries to convey it to the world. We

96

recall the Proverb: *"Speak up for those who cannot speak for themselves for the rights of all who are destitute"* (Prov. 31:8).

The prayer to Saint Gabriel that I now pray everyday states: "Pray for me that I may proclaim your message to others and be ready to suffer for love of it. . . . Give me a personal and devoted love for the word of God." When the partial birth abortion vote comes to the floor of the US Senate for the third time, your Daddy needs to proclaim God's message for life with even more strength and devotion to the cause.

Lord, please give us Your strength as we try to educate the public on the partial birth abortion issue. We pray that by sharing our story, we will be able to change a few hearts and minds. We trust in You, Lord, and know that our strong devotion to You will get us through this most difficult time.

$\mathscr{T}$HURSDAY, OCTOBER 17, 1996

Blessed are they who mourn for they will be comforted.
(Mt. 5:4)

$\mathscr{T}$ received today in the mail what was intended to be a sympathy card, but was one of the cruelest things I've ever read. The message read, "God decided to take Gabriel and you must live with it. Life goes on and adjustments are made." How could someone be so cold-hearted? I immediately called my parents who helped calm me down.

I remember reading in one of the many books I've read on surviving the death of a baby that most bereaved parents have to endure some insensitive statements. Up until now people have been so wonderful and supportive. We've received thousands of cards with such outpourings of grief. The only insensitive comment made so far had been, "Well, you have three other children." I thought that was bad, but now reading this card only adds to the pain.

I know "life goes on." Every day I wake up early in the morning to begin another day of caring for three children, all under the age of five. I'm trying so hard to keep their lives as normal and as happy as possible when my life has fallen apart.

I've learned that grieving is a process your Daddy and I must go through. It will take time. I will not allow anyone to belittle your importance in our lives. I will not let anyone make me feel that I should bury my feelings and forget about you and how much you were loved. And so I will pray for this person to understand in some small way the depth of our loss. I will also pray that God will help me to remove this anger from my heart.

Later in the day my dear friend Nadine Maenza called. Her timing is always perfect. It was such a comfort talking with her. She has been so helpful during this time. She's always there to listen and talk and care. It helps so much hearing someone say, "It's okay to cry, it's okay to feel this intense pain. It's okay to be angry. It's important for you to grieve now and go through the process, as painful as it is." She has been a true friend through this nightmare. She and her husband, Terry, sent Daddy and me two books and a heartfelt note in the hospital. Nadine and Terry know too well the heartache in losing a precious baby. They lost their beautiful little girl, Angela, at birth on March 2, 1995. I thank God for giving Nadine the courage and strength to reach out and comfort someone else in grief.

Lord, I know that You are here comforting us in our pain. You have given us strength. Please continue to help Rick and me during this time of sorrow.

*M*ONDAY, OCTOBER 21, 1996

Pleasing words are a honeycomb, sweet to the taste and
healthful to the body.
(Prv. 16:24)

*D*addy and I have been held together by the love, devotion, and prayers of so many of our friends and members of our families. We have a freezer full of meals and a house full of flowers that were all delivered with comforting visits from friends, filled with words of support, hugs, and many tears. Words cannot begin to express what those visits meant to us and how much they helped.

Today's visit, however, was filled with moments that I will remember for the rest of my life. It began when I was sitting in our family room reading to Elizabeth, Johnny, and Daniel who were all seated on my lap or right next to me. Elizabeth said she saw a car pull into the driveway. We were not expecting any visits today, and so I could not imagine who it could be. Before I got up from the chair with the children, the doorbell rang.

It was my dear friend Fran DeWine and her adorable four-year-old daughter, Anna. It was such a nice surprise. As soon as Fran came through the door she gave me a big hug and when I began to cry, she cried with me.

We went into the kitchen where she unpacked two full meals, complete with homemade bread and an apple pie. She was speaking so tenderly to the children, as she always does, telling them she had something special for them to do and pulled out some home-made dough from a bag. Elizabeth, Johnny, and even Daniel, love helping me bake, so they were really excited, wondering what we were going to do today. Then Fran pulled out cinnamon and sugar, and the children smiled and giggled as she told them we were making cinnamon rolls! It's one of their favorite things to make!

Fran put the dough into the heated oven for it to rise and the children played as Fran and I talked over a cup of tea about you and the pain involved with the loss of a child. Fran knows the sorrow that only a parent feels in the loss of a child, because she and her husband, Mike, lost their beautiful daughter, Becky DeWine.

Becky was twenty-two years old when the Lord called her home on August 4, 1993. Becky's love and gift of life continue to live on in Fran, Mike (who is a Senator from Ohio), and their children. As Fran and I sat at the table, we talked all about you and the impact of your brief life and about Becky and the impact of her twenty-two years.

Fran said that as difficult as it has been and continues to be, she thanks God for the years she was blessed with the life of her dear daughter. She spoke of so many memories with Becky that she will forever cherish and remember. I will never forget Fran saying that she thought the loss of a baby was in a way more difficult because you never had the time to know your child. She said that it's sad that parents who lose infants must suffer the pain of what will never be—the cries, laughter, smiles, touch, and all of the rich moments that make memories. Fran went on to say that she knew people at times will under-

101

mine the loss when it involves the death of a baby, especially a preemie, and she thought this was so unfortunate.

It was also wonderful talking to Fran about you, Gabriel. I love talking about you! I want to talk about you, but too often people stand in silence and don't mention you or your name. I know it's because they are uncomfortable and not sure of what to say or how to talk with a grieving mother.

I was so impressed that Fran was able to reach out and comfort me in such a special way. She knows grief too well, and she did not minimize my grief because you died so young. Rather, she acknowledged it, understood it, and felt it in such a heartfelt way. I will never forget her kindness.

Fran and I talked and cried and even laughed together for a long time. After a while, when the bread dough had risen, we all made a loaf of bread and cinnamon rolls with the children. I cannot begin to express the joy the children had in playing with Anna and making those delicious cinnamon rolls.

That visit from Fran was a welcome ray of sunshine.

Lord, thank You for giving Fran the strength to speak from her heart with such heartfelt concern and love. Please help me to have the strength to help other grieving parents in their times of need. Thank You for such wonderful friends.

THURSDAY, OCTOBER 24, 1996

What he commanded our ancestors, they were to teach their children; That the next generation might come to know, children yet to be born. In turn they were to recite them to their children, that they too might put their trust in God, And not forget the works of God, keeping his commandments.
(Ps. 78:5–7)

Throughout the partial birth abortion debate, through all the distortions, all the untruths, all the back and forth between both sides, one very compelling image remained, I think, in the minds of many Americans. That image was of a very sick infant destined to die shortly after birth and the anguished parents who thought they had no choice but to end their child's life with a partial birth abortion. This image became the fault line of the whole debate, the so called "hard cases" argument used by its supporters, the supposed reason for sanctioning this procedure.

Gabriel, I wish we could take that image—the image of agonized parents compelled to chose virtual infanticide—and replace it with the image we knew.

When you were born and lived for two hours, something simple but profound happened. Your Daddy and I became the parents of a newborn baby and welcomed you into our family.

That was all.

But that was everything.

In two hours, we experienced life as deeply, as intensely

103

as we might have in an entire lifetime. The emotions that make up a life—love, sorrow, regret, joy—were packed into the brief span of time that was your own life. The life of Gabriel Michael Santorum. To have rejected that experience, to have tried to cut ourselves off from that through the partial birth procedure, would have been to reject your life and the beauty of all life.

Gabriel, I wish that everyone who will face the circumstances that we did might know how much that time with you meant to us. As emotional as it was, fighting for your life and having whatever time we could with you meant everything to your Daddy and me. It was not only being able to be there for you, loving and caring for you, but it was also acknowledging you as a child of God and as a person who lived and died.

During the debate a Senator said, "If these babies were to survive, we know from testimony they would live moments, maybe seconds . . . . " How could parents give up an opportunity for love, no matter how brief, in exchange for such violence? I believe it's simply because pro-abortion activists do not want women to know the truth. I listened carefully to the debate and sadly watched as the Senators supporting partial birth abortion distorted the truth and deceived the public. When we learn of the details of what a partial birth abortion is—the terrible cold-blooded brutality of it—everything inside of us cries out for a different solution, for a better way. And in response to that cry, we are told that there is no other way.

There is another way. We know, because we chose it. It was to deliver you and allow you to die a natural and peaceful death in the loving arms of your parents. If only this image

104

could replace the image I mentioned above—that of parents who chose a brutal, painful procedure when it isn't necessary—I think we could expand this discussion to include a very real alternative. To suggest that there simply are not any is to suffocate our own humanity. It is to compel us to be less than what we are. It is to take what is deep and profound and mysterious about being human and cut it off by means of a merciless "procedure." There can be no crueler deception than this.

Accepting partial birth abortion as our only alternative to a difficult birth or a potentially disabled infant is to thwart two of our strongest human needs: Those of love and memory. Giving life to and caring for a sick infant—for however brief a period—allows us to express these uniquely human needs. Daddy and I were blessed with the time to offer the fullness of our love to you, Gabriel, and we have the peace of knowing that you felt that love. You joined our family forever. You have not been obliterated. You were known and will always be remembered. Your memory lives within us always.

I thank God that I will always be able to recall the memories of our time together—cradling you inside me, holding you in my arms, and touching your soft face. I thank God that the image of your beautiful face and delicate little body will be imprinted on my heart and mind forever. And I thank God for the treasured keepsakes—your pictures, your little hat, undershirt and blanket, your little handprints and footprints.

Memory helps anchor us to each other. It locates us not only within a certain time and place, but within a community and within a family. It is one of the measures of the value we place upon one another. Daddy and I believe that every human being should be remembered by someone.

Lord, we pray that parents will open up their hearts to Your wisdom and embrace the life of their unborn. For it is in living with the grace of Your Holy Spirit that we are filled with Your love of all life and will follow Your commands. Bless all of our children, those living and those yet to be born, and help us to teach them Your ways - for all generations to come.

FRIDAY, NOVEMBER 1, 1996

At that time the disciples approached Jesus and said,
"Who is the greatest in the kingdom of heaven?"
He called a child over, placed it in their midst,
and said, "Amen, I say to you, unless you turn and
become like children, you will not enter the kingdom of
heaven. Whoever humbles himself like this child is the
greatest in the kingdom of heaven.
(Mt. 18:1–4)

Today is All Saints Day—it's your day! I try to go to daily mass as often as I can. It helps me in everything I do, and it keeps me focused on what's really important. I think of you all the time now—especially when I'm at mass. Your spirit is forever present in my life. We feel you in the inspiring words of our prayers, in the gentle breeze that cools us and the sunshine that warms our faces. Gabriel, you are with us always.

Elizabeth and Johnny include you in our prayers every day. As we were driving home from mass today, Elizabeth and Johnny talked about their guardian angels and how lucky they were to have an extra one watching over them—you! They asked if we could have cake and ice cream every year on your birthday to celebrate your life. Of course! What a beautiful thing to do! One evening in the wee hours of the night, Elizabeth woke up frightened, and, instead of coming to our room, she fell back to sleep. She explained the next morning it was because she prayed for you to be with her, Gabriel, and "he helped me not to be afraid and to fall back to sleep." It's wonderful that your siblings have this awareness of you—and hopefully always will as they travel through life.

Lord, thank You so much for my beautiful children with their sweet faces and innocent remarks. Please help me teach them Your ways and keep them away from sin. I pray that I, too, may be more childlike and the kind of mother You want me to be.

*M*ONDAY, NOVEMBER 11, 1996

*Blessed is the man who trusts in the Lord, whose confidence
is in him. He will be like a tree planted by the water that
sends out its roots by the stream. It does not fear when heat
comes; its leaves are always green. It has no worries in a
year of drought and never fails to bear fruit.*
(Jer. 17:7)

*I*t's already one month since you died. Daddy and I are slowly working our way through the grieving process. It's painful, and its long, and there are times when I wish I could give this pain to someone else for just a day. Daddy says it's so difficult when he is out working in so many areas of the state. He's always having to maintain an outward composure. On the outside he smiles and acts like he's fine, but he carries within him a heavy heart and too frequently has to hold back the tears.

I often find myself missing you so much, wanting you back, wanting to hold you. And it's during these moments that I fall apart. Yesterday, Elizabeth asked, "Mommy, if Gabriel is in heaven, then why are you crying?" She was right. At moments like that, I need to pull myself back into the spiritual realm, and I find comfort in knowing you are in God's eternal care.

*God, help me to focus on the blessedness of my little one. I
know You have prepared a special place for Gabriel in heaven.
Help me to strengthen my faith, and to never lose my trust in You.*

109

FRIDAY, NOVEMBER 22, 1996

Amen, amen, I say to you, unless a grain
of wheat falls to the ground and dies, it remains
just a grain of wheat; but if it dies, it produces
much fruit. Whoever loves his life loses it, and
whoever hates his life in this world will preserve
it for eternal life. Whoever serves me must follow me,
and where I am, there also will my servant be.
The Father will honor whoever serves me.
(Jn. 12:24–26)

I made a beautiful angel wreath for your grave. Nadine gave me the idea, and I really appreciated her suggestions. I've made a lot of wreaths for our home; there's one in almost every room. An angel wreath was perfect for you, and I must admit it is so pretty. I put a lot of time into making this wreath for you. It's the only way that I can mother you. It's so sad, but it helps me to feel like I'm doing something for you, my dear son.

Your grave was still blanketed with flowers so we rearranged them and added the wreath. I sat on the ground that covers you—our special piece of earth—and cried. Daddy and I have ordered you a monument, but it is not ready yet. It will be nice to have your grave marked, but then again, it breaks my heart.

*D*o not stand at my grave and weep;
  I am not there. I do not sleep.

  I am a thousand winds that blow.
  I am the diamond glints on snow.
  I am the sunlight in ripened grain.
  I am the gentle autumn's rain.

When you awaken in the morning's hush,
  I am the sweet uplifting rush
  of quiet birds in circled flight.
I am the soft stars that shine at night.

  Do not stand at my grave and cry;
  I am not there. I did not die.

ANONYMOUS

Lord, teach me Your ways, and fill me with Your Spirit.
Thank you for being here with our family.

*One thing I ask of the Lord; this I seek: To dwell in the Lord's house
all the days of my life, To gaze on the Lord's beauty,
to visit his temple. For God will hide me in his shelter in time of
trouble, Will conceal me in the cover of his tent;
and set me high upon a rock.*
(Ps. 27:4–5)

*But we hold this treasure in earthen vessels, that the surpassing power
may be of God and not from us. We are afflicted in every way, but
not constrained; perplexed, but not driven to despair; persecuted, but
not abandoned; struck down, but not destroyed; always carrying about
in the body the dying of Jesus, so that the life of Jesus may also be
manifested in our body. For we who live are constantly being given
up to death for the sake of Jesus, so that the life of Jesus may be manifested in our mortal flesh.*
(2 Cor. 4:7–11)

$\mathscr{T}$ spoke with a friend today who I know probably had good intentions and did not mean to hurt me. She said to me, "You are so blessed. I know a family who has lost two babies and just had another with a birth defect." How cruel for anyone to try and minimize my loss by telling me stories of worse tragedies! How cruel for anyone to try and undermine your meaning and significance in my life!

Some people do not recognize the depth of a parent's loss. They can't imagine how such a small person whom a parent had so little time with could leave such a huge void. They want parents to quickly get over their child's death and put it behind them. I find it so strange that at times it's as if some people measure a parent's pain on a graph according to what they think the intensity should be. And according to these people's calculations, the grief experienced with the loss of a twenty-week preemie is less than at forty weeks which is less than losing a six-month-old baby, and so on, and the older a child gets, the worse it is!

How outrageous. Because the truth is that the death of a child—no matter what age—is always a profound loss.

My friend Nadine summed it up so perfectly. She said, "On a scale of 1-10 losing a child, at any age, is always a 10." And she's right.

I am told by so many parents that the pain will lessen, and I will have a peace about your death someday. I have learned to integrate your loss, Gabriel, into my life, but I think there will always be a sadness and a wish that you could be with us. While I do hope this pain will lessen (because it's too much at times), I know there will be a place in my heart that will always ache for you. And that's okay. Because I never want the memory of you— beautiful you— to go away.

Lord, I know that You are here with me. Please help me find peace in moments of distress, comfort during times of pain, and strength when I am weak.

SATURDAY, DECEMBER 14, 1996

But who indeed are you, a human being, to talk back to
God? Will what is made say to its maker,
"Why have you created me so?"
(Rom. 9:20)

I call heaven and earth today to witness against you. I
have set before you life and death, the blessing and the
curse. Choose life, then, that you and your descendants
may live, by loving the Lord, your God, heeding his voice,
and holding fast to him.
(Dt. 30:19–20)

Today, I have been filled with sadness. I have been reminded
how conditional love can sometimes be. This is part of what you
did for me, Gabriel: You made me more keenly aware of how
much we can and should give to one another. You made me realize that we should never be stingy with our love. In a very personal way, you brought home to Daddy and me the truth that love,
by its very definition, can never be conditional.

What prompted these thoughts? A friend of mine told me she
was going to have an amniocentesis. My heart sank as she said
this. I asked if she knew the risk of miscarriage was high with this
procedure—one in 200—and even higher in cases where the
physician is less experienced. She said her physician disclosed the
risks and was pushing her to go ahead with the amnio. My friend

said she and her husband decided they had to have the "peace of mind" of knowing everything is fine and could not "bear the burden" if something is wrong with their baby.

I am filled with sadness for my friend because I remember too well how worry for you, Gabriel, consumed my every thought. I know so well this fear, this uncertainty. I understand too keenly the need to be reassured of a healthy baby who can live a happy, productive life.

But I have come to believe that we lose so much when we start to be selective with our acceptance and our love, both as individuals and as a society. Children are always a burden in one way or another. What happens when we start to believe that we can choose whether or not to accept the particular burdens a child brings into our lives? What happens when prenatal testing can detect if a child will develop diabetes, chronic ear infections, leukemia, or another debilitating or life-threatening disease? It worries me greatly to think that certain children could be routinely classified as too burdensome to live. Never for a moment did we think of you as a burden, Gabriel. You were our child. This has been your gift to us—you have made us understand even more deeply how important it is to accept and cherish all life, because we can lose it so swiftly. And life is always a gift, it is never ours to control, manipulate or extinguish. I can't help but think of the words of Karl Barth, the Swiss theologian who wrote so beautifully about the need to respect all life, and what our attitudes toward vulnerable life say about us:

No community whether family, village or state is really strong if it will not carry its very weakest members.

115

They belong to it no less than the strong, and the quiet work of their maintenance and care, which might seem useless on a superficial view, is perhaps more effective than common labor, culture or historical conflict in knitting it closely and securely together. On the other hand, a community which regards and treats its weak members as a hindrance, and even proceeds to their extermination, is on the verge of collapse.

KARL BARTH (1961)
Church Dogmatics, vol 3, no 4. T&T Clark, Edinburgh.

Lord, please be with parents during their pregnancies, and help each one of us to realize that all babies are beautiful creations. You know exactly what You are molding and making. Please help parents love their children unconditionally at all stages of life. Lord, help all of us as parents realize that we are honored to care for the little children You put into our lives.

TUESDAY, DECEMBER 24, 1996

Let not kindness and fidelity leave you; bind them around
your neck; Then you will win favor and good
esteem before God and man.
(Prv. 3:3–4)

Lord, my heart is not proud; nor are my eyes haughty.
I do not busy myself with great matters,
with things too sublime for me.
(Ps. 131:1)

It's Christmas Eve. The children are all tucked warmly into
bed. The season has been truly beautiful. We decorated the
house, as usual, the weekend after Thanksgiving.

There are two very special ornaments hanging on the
Christmas tree in honor of you, Gabriel. One is your sweet picture and the other is St. Gabriel the Archangel. The nativity set is
on the dining room table. The gingerbread house we made with
the children is sitting in the kitchen. The needlepoint stockings
are hanging on the fireplace where Santa's cookies are placed, and
the tree and Christmas books are in the living room—or as we
refer to it at this time of year, the Christmas room.

Daddy has been home almost every night for dinner these
last two months, and he took a couple of weeks off to be with us
over the holiday. It's been wonderful having him home. Daddy
usually has the energy of about ten people, but since your death,

he's been melancholy. Being with me, Elizabeth, Johnny, and Daniel helps cheer him up. We've spent a lot of time together these past few weeks listening to Christmas music, drinking hot cocoa, reading Christmas stories, playing games and singing carols in front of the tree.

For the first time in my life, I had all of my shopping done and gifts wrapped early. Ever since you left us, I have kept myself extra busy. It helps me get through the long lonely days. I have wonderful days with your sister and brothers—we have a splendid life together—but I continue to live with a sadness within my heart simply because I miss you so much.

So here we are this Christmas Eve. It's a silent night, it's a holy night, but it's also another evening we're painfully reminded that you are physically gone from our lives. We miss you, Gabriel.

The hour is late. Daddy and I have been busy putting the children's wooden castle and dollhouse and car garage together. After arranging the toys and eating Santa's cookies, Daddy and I opened our gifts to each other. They're very different this year. After a long search, we bought each other St. Gabriel and St. Michael statues in honor of your life. They are extremely beautiful and one of a kind. Both were handmade in Northern Italy, close to PopPop's hometown. Before going to bed Daddy and I talked for a while. We had another long talk about you and how you've changed our lives.

Ever since I've known him, your Daddy has always been there for me and our children. He is a man who is totally devoted to the sacredness of our marriage and family life. Daddy and I have always been blessed with a marriage full of understanding, love, and affection.

But losing you, Gabriel, has brought us even closer, and our marriage now has a new dimension. "Being there" for each other in this time of sadness and supporting each other through the pain has been a great source of comfort to us both. Your Daddy's love soothes and warms my broken heart. Losing you, Gabriel, was a tragedy Daddy and I went through together. The circle of life and death has never touched our lives so deeply. You were our flesh and blood, and so together we have mourned your loss in a most intimate way.

The loss of you, Gabriel, has also reaffirmed our beliefs as parents. Daddy and I have always realized that we will have only one chance to raise our children. In a world where people too frequently put their work, positions, and egos above their children, we know it's important to remember that there is only one chance. Only one chance to capture all of the beautiful moments, only one chance to be there for our children, only one chance to raise good children. We think of the psalmist saying, *"Teach us to count our days aright, that we may gain wisdom of heart." (Ps.90:12)*

Losing you, Gabriel, has reinforced in Daddy and me the desire to capture all the moments with our children because life here on earth passes by so quickly.

Lord, help me to always be a kind, gentle, and loving mother. Help me to remain focused on the important role I play in each of my children's lives. Please encourage me, Lord, in my daily work as I raise my children, and help me realize that each day with my children is a precious gift from You. You have so blessed me with their lives. For it is this day and every day that I should love and enjoy my dear children. I pray that my children will know You and walk in Your ways.

$\mathcal{T}$UESDAY, DECEMBER 31, 1996

The Lord is my shepherd; there is nothing I lack.
In green pastures you let me graze; to safe waters
you lead me; you restore my strength.
You guide me along the right path for the sake of your
name. Even when I walk through a dark valley,
I fear no harm for you are at my side;
your rod and staff give me courage.
(Ps. 23:1–4)

$\mathcal{T}$his is the last evening for the year 1996. Daddy and I decided to spend it quietly at home with the children. While reflecting on this past year we keep returning to thoughts of you. You were our 1996: the great news that we were expecting you, our pregnancy together, your life within me, your anomaly, our surgery, your birth, your death—and your new life in heaven.

It is difficult starting a new year without you, especially since your birth was going to be the highlight of 1997. Daddy and I know that God allowed our situation to occur; He allowed us to feel completely helpless and powerless, just like He allowed His only son to feel completely powerless nailed to the cross.

But we must remember that it was at that moment of Christ's powerlessness when the immense power of the crucifixion was released and salvation was brought to the world. Someday God will reveal how our tragedy was for His glory. Through the suffering Daddy and I have endured we have come

120

to a more devoted and deeper relationship with God. In your death you were born to a new life with Jesus, and we, too, were born to a new life spiritually. Your death has renewed our faith, and heaven means even more to us now.

Lord, Gabriel was our tender little lamb, and You reached into the flock and picked him up. We know that he is up in heaven calling us ~ with Jesus ~ asking us to climb the rocky mountain of life. For all the rest of our days, Daddy and I will follow You, the Great Shepherd who has our little Gabriel cradled so beautifully in His arms. We begin this new year even more devoted to our lives in Christ. Thank You, Lord, for helping to lead us closer to eternal life with You.

We do not want you to be unaware, brothers, about those who have fallen asleep, so that you may not grieve like the rest, who have no hope. For if we believe that Jesus died and rose, so too will God, through Jesus, bring with him those who have fallen asleep. . . . Then we who are alive, who are left, will be caught up together with them in the clouds to meet the Lord in the air. Thus, we shall always be with the Lord.
(1 Thes. 4:13–14, 17)

*T*oday is a bittersweet day. It's your due date, and my mind keeps returning to thoughts of you and how wonderful this day would have been if only I could still have you. But it's also a happy day in that I remind myself to smile and rejoice in the knowledge that you, Gabriel, are being loved by God more than Daddy and I could ever imagine.

Grandma and Granddad called today, as did my siblings and friend Nadine. I was outside enjoying some sunshine and a walk with the children when they called. Their heartfelt messages on our answering machine meant so much that I replayed them a few times.

While outside, the children like to look up at the clouds and tell me what they see. Johnny saw a "long neck dinosaur," and Elizabeth "an elephant." A few minutes later, as I was drawing them a hopscotch on the drive, Elizabeth looked into the sky and said, "Mommy look, there's a cloud with wings—it's a Gabriel cloud!"

Yes, it was a Gabriel cloud! And you are there in the clouds and in the breeze and in the sun that lights our days and in the moon that lights our nights. You are with us always, little Gabriel. You will always be a part of our family, and we all look forward to being with you in heaven someday for all eternity.

Lord, You have prepared a place for our child with You in heaven. We know that You took from our family to build Your family. Like You, my little Gabriel is reaching out his hands to us and calling us to come and be with him. Lord, we pray we will have eternal life with You, Gabriel, and all of our relatives someday.

Your Birthday . . .

SATURDAY, OCTOBER 11, 1997

To every thing there is a season,
and a time to every purpose under the heaven:
A time to be born, and a time to die; a time to plant,
and a time to pluck up that which is planted.
(Eccl. 3: 1–2)

Today is the one year anniversary of your birth and your death. After losing you it seemed as though the sun would never rise and the stars would never again sparkle in the night sky. But the sun continued to light the earth—and the twinkle of each night star still offered a promise of hope. It seemed so cruel at the time for nature and every part of the world to keep moving with its normal rhythms when my life had stopped.

The seasons have changed four times since your death. The grave where you rest has been covered in the colorful leaves of autumn, blanketed white with snow, and has brought forth new life in the blossoms of spring and summer flowers. Usually the change of the seasons brought joy and hope, and then I found the cyclic quality reassuring. I could count on the repetition, on the reappearance of each season at its appointed time.

But now, as the cycle repeats itself, it just takes me further and further from you and from the brief time I had with you. With each passing fall, winter, spring, and summer, I am reminded that there is another season between us.

The season of spring, with its new life evident in every small bud on the trees and bulbs peeking up through the ground adding their splashes of color, had an even deeper meaning for your Daddy and me. This year, the spring had a special, bittersweet meaning for all of our family. There was also a new life beginning in me.

How appropriate that the cold dark winter—lifeless and bleak—should follow your death. Through the healing eventually came spring, the season when days become brighter, air becomes warmer, and hope is seen in every new life—on the trees, in the flowers, and yes, within me. I am expecting a new baby.

When your Daddy and I found out we were expecting again, the feelings of excitement we always felt in the past were now clouded with some fear about the unknown. We thanked God again and again for this gift. But, at the same time, this moment sadly reminded us of you. We had questions. Death is now very real to me. I lost you. I could lose a baby again. The thought of that is almost too much to bear.

Daddy and I waited longer this time before announcing the news. You are still so much with us, and I didn't want anyone to think we were moving on without you, Gabriel. While life continues on, we will always move on with you ever present in our lives.

After losing you, Gabriel, I wanted to wait a long time before even considering becoming pregnant again. No one else could take your place. I ached for you, and my womb was meant only for you until your due date. However, while no one could ever possibly take your special place in our lives, with time Daddy and I started, painfully, to accept your death. The process of arriving at this acceptance and this peace was long and diffi-

125

cult. Creating new life is like that—for that is what Daddy and I were doing. We were slowly creating our lives and ourselves anew, to rejuvenate those parts of our hearts that died with you.

With the beginning of a new year, I began to realize that having another child was not a betrayal. Resisting new life, refusing rebirth in any way—be it another child or simply the rebirth in our hearts—would not bring you back. I began to realize that you—perfect now in Heaven—could only feel joy and happiness for your parents if we were to conceive another child. With time, Daddy and I knew we wanted another child, and we prayed for another child. Our prayers were answered on April 22, my birthday gift from God.

I began to see new life all around me. The spring mirrored my own rebirth—and the start of this new life. And I saw exuberant life most closely and joyfully in Elizabeth, Johnny, and Daniel. During these spring days, so sunny and clear, they spent most of their time outdoors as I pushed them on their swings, filled their sandbox toys, and watched them ride their bikes. Summer came quickly with its hot humid days, but we always managed to find a piece of cool grass under a shady tree, and the sprinkler made for a lot of fun afternoons with the children.

Gradually, with the difficult passing of this year, I realize that my memories of you won't be tied to the seasons. You will always be with us. We still include you in every prayer, and your pictures will always remain next to your siblings throughout our home.

My love for this new baby is strong and deep. I know how blessed I am. Daddy and I love this baby intensely and are so excited about loving and caring for him or her. This is what love is. It is watching your sister and brothers at summer play, it is loving a new baby before birth.

And life is also fragile, more so than I ever knew until I had you, Gabriel. I realize, too, that during pregnancy, when life is at its fullest and most miraculous, it is also at its most delicate. In retrospect, I think I took my first four pregnancies for granted, even though I was awed by what was happening within me. With each pregnancy, I prayed for that child every day and followed the development week by week, but I always assumed my baby would be healthy, because I was so healthy.

Now it's different. After losing you, I now realize how delicate and fragile a time pregnancy is. Something can go wrong at any time. I can take the best care of myself, follow all of the prenatal guidelines for a healthy pregnancy offered by my physician and in the medical books, and I could still lose my baby. As I learned with you, my little one, ultimately it is out of my control.

I keep telling myself that "everything is fine" with this new baby, and "most babies are healthy." But this hope and reassurance is all faded with the thought that you had a fatal defect that rarely occurs, and so referring to numbers on charts and statistics in books is no reassurance to me. The only reassurance for your Daddy and me is our faith in God. I have learned to surrender even more to His protection and care.

My faith in God's goodness is what has kept me so calm and relaxed through most of this pregnancy. In the past I always prayed to God for healthy babies. Now, there is a second part of my prayer for a healthy baby, and it's asking God to give me

127

courage and fortitude to accept with grace whatever God presents to us.

The only unsettling part of this pregnancy was between eighteen and twenty weeks. Since that's when we lost you, Gabriel, those weeks were filled with many tears. All the memories surrounding your death came rushing back in vivid detail. I thought so much about you and I worried about the baby inside me.

By eighteen weeks I had not yet felt any movement—not even that butterfly feeling—and I thought of you. I sat quietly hoping to feel something, but there was nothing. I wanted so much to feel a kick from this little one in me, so much that I would lie awake at night waiting for that first sign of life. I kept thinking of you and feared the nightmare was happening all over again.

My doctor, Camilla Hersh, was wonderful when I called her first thing on a Sunday morning! I had myself convinced there was something terribly wrong. Dr. Hersh calmed me, and we spoke for a while. She described my feelings as a type of "anniversary reaction" which is common after one loses a baby, but an important feeling to pay attention to. Dr. Hersh said this is a sadness that will come from time to time. We want to make sure the child I'm carrying is fine, but it's all right to revisit the emotions surrounding the loss of a loved one—especially when it's a baby.

We also spoke about the need to have faith and pray in order to find peace. Dr. Hersh then told me what to do to try and feel the baby move, and lo and behold, for the first time I felt this baby move! It was such a beautiful feeling, and I was so happy Daddy was there to share the moment.

It was a while ago when I felt that first little kick. I am now thirty weeks pregnant and loving every day as I care for Elizabeth, Johnny, Daniel, and this new baby in me. He or she is an active baby, turning and kicking all throughout the day and late at night! Every time the baby kicks me it's as if to say, "Mommy, everything's all right."

Like the changing seasons, there have been changes occurring in me physically to nurture this delicate life. All take place over time with my body adjusting to every intricate detail of my baby's needs in order to protect and sustain this beautiful new life. I marvel at the miracle of a baby.

A few weeks ago we began the season of fall. The world has brightened full of color high above the faded flowers. Shades of red, gold and autumn orange delight our eyes. And when the color of the leaves dulls to tones of brown falling dry and lifeless upon the earth, it will fill our hearts with excitement as we prepare for the birth of our child. Unlike the cold dark winter of last year, hopefully this one will be filled with much happiness, warmth, and brighter days.

Dear Lord, please help me to be aware of Your presence through every changing season of my life. Humble me in happy times, and help me to embrace the cross in times of despair. You are my strength and my rock. Please continue to bless Rick, Elizabeth, Johnny, Daniel, Gabriel in heaven, and my baby on the way. Lord, with each day help me to be a good wife and mother, full of patience, love and kindness.

*Jesus turned to them and said, "Daughters of Jerusalem,
do not weep for me; weep instead for yourselves and for
your children, for indeed, the days are coming when
people will say, Blessed are the barren, the wombs that
never bore and the breasts that never nursed."
(Lk. 23:27–29)*

Gabriel, I have thought so much about you this weekend. I cried as I looked through the special basket of things that touched you. Your baby blanket, hat, and tiny footprints were all held with much affection. It was a blue weekend, but as Daddy and I planted flowers at your grave, we realized there is a peace in knowing you are indeed a part of God's eternal plan.

On Friday evening, Daddy and I received a call from his Washington office telling us that the President had vetoed the partial birth abortion ban. We were with Grandma and Granddad sitting in their front yard at the time. I took the call and could hardly believe what I was hearing. Though I expected a veto, I thought it almost eerie for this to have been signed at the close of business on the eve of your one year birthday. When I hung up and told your Daddy the news, he shook his head and cracked a wry smile. We looked at each other knowing what the other was thinking. The irony was not lost on either of us.

But then I thought about what Jesus said about having faith and not allowing our hearts to be troubled, but rather to listen for God's

130

message. God speaks to us in so many ways. He's there speaking; we can hear Him if we just open up our hearts and let Him into our lives.

So much has happened that I cannot begin to understand since last year. One occurrence goes through my mind so many times. During the partial birth abortion debate, a Senator was thanking the women who had had partial birth abortions for coming forward with their stories. She said, ". . . they are crying. They are crying because they do not understand how Senators could take away an option . . . They are crying because they do not believe that those Senators truly understand what this meant for their families . . ."

Daddy said in response, "The Senator . . . said she hears the cries of the women outside this Chamber. We would be deafened by the cries of the children who are not here to cry because of this procedure."

The Washington Post described what happened next. "Republican Sen. Rick Santorum turned to face the opposition and in a high, pleading voice cried out, "Where do we draw the line? Some people have likened this procedure to an appendectomy. That's not an appendix," he shouted, pointing to a drawing of a fetus. "That is not a blob of tissue. It is a baby. It's a baby."

"And then, impossibly, in an already hushed gallery, in one of those moments when the floor of the Senate looks like a stage set, with its small wooden desks somehow too small for the matters at hand, the cry of a baby pierced the room, echoing across the chamber from an outside hallway. No one mentioned the cry, but for a few seconds, no one spoke at all."

A coincidence? Perhaps . . . a visitor's baby was crying just as the door to the floor of the Senate was opened, then closed. Or maybe

131

. . . it was a cry from the son whose voice we never heard, but whose life has forever changed ours.

I'll Always Love You,

Mommy